Starting Over

A Practical Guide
For Reinventing
Your Career
In Midlife

RAJAN CHOPRA

Starting Over © Copyright 2020 by Rajan Chopra

ISBN: 978-1-7353812-0-6 (paperback)
ISBN: 978-1-7353812-1-3 (ebook)

Dedicated to all who dream of a better life,
have the courage to change,
the will to persevere,
and the heart to give back
when eventual success is found.

Acknowledgments

This book was born from the desire to lend a helping hand of sorts and share insights, observations, and experiences to provide inspiration for those who may be struggling to find their way in life. I am grateful to many, many people who have been a positive force in my life, and who at one time or another were supportive influences in my careers and the writing of this book.

I am thankful to my deceased parents, Pramila and Ved Chopra, for having provided much love and the best education they could afford. I am thankful to my sister, Poonam Kapoor, for her lifelong, unconditional love and support. I am thankful to my son, Kabir Chopra, for his love, insights, and encouragement. I am grateful to Sandeep Mathrani, who gave me my first break in getting my coaching practice off the ground; to David McCourt for being a dear friend and mentor; to Rupi Puri for helping me get into a trading career; to Andy Carlson and Tony Hamer for being great friends and supporters; to Sanjay Sathe for being a great friend and inspiring thinker; and to many, many coaching clients who entrusted me.

The book would not have been possible without the love, encouragement, and unrelenting support of Trish Blasi, my partner in life. I am thankful to her. Finally, I am grateful to my editor, Samantha Mason, for expertly guiding me in the development of this book with thoughtful ideas and extraordinary editorial skills to make a first-time author's dream a reality.

Foreword

I f I could think of one person to write a book on reinventing careers, that person would be Rajan Chopra. He has walked the walk by reinventing his own career four times in over four decades. He knows what it takes to remake oneself and shares his practical insights and wisdom in this book.

I have been described as a serial entrepreneur – in fact, Ernst and Young once awarded me their 'Entrepreneur of the Year' award. So, you could say I know a thing or two about inventing new businesses, as well as reinventing oneself. I have founded or acquired over 25 companies all over the globe. Reinvention has been key in my life. 'A Total Rethink' is a theme in my own personal journey, the title of my book, and a position not unlike Raj's. I can say with absolute certainty that change is inevitable, to be ready and flexible when it comes is key, herein lies sound strategies for survival and a new way forward.

Rajan and I first met over 20 years ago, back when the new telecom and dot.com era was taking off, and there were huge opportunities in the emerging internet economy. Naturally, I seized the opportunity and started a new telecom company to build fiber optic networks to provide last mile connectivity for consumers. Rajan, at the time, was working on Wall Street, and I convinced him to quit his finance job and join my team as I led the telecom revolution.

When I heard Raj was going to write a book about career reinvention, I knew it was going to be spot on. After all, he has his own history to draw on. Both he and I have lived through many career changes, both planned and unplanned, and only a person who has actually been there can explain what it is really like in a believable manner. Little did I then realize the timeliness of such an effort. *Starting Over* has never been a more important subject than during today's unsettling and turbulent times. Even before the current difficulties, jobs had been rapidly changing, evolving, and disappearing through the disruptive change brought on by technological innovations. But today, it is difficult to overstate the magnitude of job displacement worldwide where an exogenous event like the COVID pandemic accelerates the pace of creative disruption. Reinvention isn't just a nice-sounding idea. Instead, it is suddenly paramount to millions of people. Old ways of operating may be simply going away, perhaps for good. We are left wondering what will become of sports, concerts, and cruises. There are so many unanswered questions. Thankfully, a person like Rajan can interject some positivity into all this. He sees an enormous silver lining in the world's troubles because he realizes that disruption always brings new opportunities. As someone who has personally reinvented his own career no fewer than four times, he is a person worth listening to. His last career reinvention happened in his mid-60s. As he has both said and demonstrated, age is not important. The challenges may differ along each stage of life, but he has proven it can always be done.

This book is a practical guide to teach the reader, step by step, how to do it as well. Rajan has written detailed roadmaps outlining each key topic, from how to plan a new career, through executing that plan, and even how to handle both success and failure of your plan. Detailed analysis of important research is shown, backed up by pertinent real-life examples. He has many useful cases of what he and others did during some very difficult and anxious times. Importantly, not everything he did worked as planned, and he explains what happened in those situations as well.

Rajan is overall a realist and does not sugar-coat the difficult parts. Having experienced transitions more than once, he knows personally that changes take time and how best to plan for that, as well as explaining ways to make incremental steps onward to eventual success. His is not a book that provides an overnight formula where you instantly step into a fabulous new career. This book is for the serious person who is motivated to put in the effort and work to attain the reward. As he freely admits, "reinvention requires hard work," but with Rajan's contagious optimism and life lessons at your side, at least some of the hard work has already been done. If your career needs a reboot or a big change, or even if you need a completely new one, you could do no better than using Rajan and *Starting Over* to put you back on the path to a fulfilling life. I highly recommend reading it.

—David C. McCourt Chairman and CEO of Granahan McCourt Capital, Chairman of National Broadband Ireland, and author of *Total Rethink: Why Entrepreneurs Should Act Like Revolutionaries.*

Table of Contents

Introduction

There has rarely been a more opportune time to reinvent your career than now.

Congratulations on seeking help in starting your journey to a new career because it can be scary and overwhelming. I will be the first to tell you that this process requires work and dedication but, in *Starting Over*, I show you how to overcome the challenges and reinvent yourself and your career. Your age and experience do not matter when it comes to remaking yourself. Whether you are a middle-aged manager, executive, life-long company veteran, or independent professional, it is never too early or too late to make a change and reinvent yourself.

How do I know? Because I have successfully reinvented my own career four times over a period of four decades and learned what works – and what does not – in the process of successful career reinventions. I went from being a broke immigrant from India to becoming an audit professional with PricewaterhouseCoopers in Sweden, a derivatives trader with JPMorgan Chase on Wall Street, co-founding business start-ups, and a certified executive coach at the age of 65. I am now enjoying some of the best years of my life. If I can reinvent my career and be successful, so can you.

In *Starting Over*, I guide you with simple, practical steps on how to overcome the challenges that you face and remake your career to the life you desire, where you can be emotionally satisfied and financially secure. I am a certified executive coach and have spent a lifetime guiding and helping hundreds of professionals with their careers – young associates, mid-level managers, senior executives, CEOs, and entrepreneurs.

This book comprises essential principles and action steps that are simple to understand, which is the easy part. The hard part is in the execution of the action steps – the actual work that you must do when making the transition. *Starting Over* provides the tools, but it is up to you to put them into action.

For example, you may hire a personal trainer to help you buff up, increase stamina, or get into better physical shape. That is a great first step. While the trainer will be your accountability partner and cheerleader, design your exercise regimen for the gym, and encourage you to eat healthy foods, it is *you* who must do the heavy lifting. You must show up at the gym five days a week and religiously work out according to the plan. Only then, perhaps six months down the road, will you see the results. Without putting in the work, even the best-conceived plans will simply remain wishful thinking. It is the same for the process of reinventing our careers.

To be sure, reinvention requires hard work, but the process becomes less onerous when it is broken down into steps akin to solving any other problem.

First, recognize that there is a problem with your current job or career for which you want to find a solution. Begin by identifying what the problem is. Here are a few common causes for contemplating a career change:

1. Have you lost your job?
2. Do you feel stuck in your career?

3. Are you frustrated and feel stressed at work?

4. Is your career at risk?

5. Are you contemplating a career change?

6. Did technological innovations make your skills obsolete?

7. Have other disruptive forces negatively impacted your industry?

Causes (6) and (7), relating to skills obsolescence and industry disruption, are the more difficult reinventions because they usually require new education or training. And, these are the primary reasons why many will have to rethink and reinvent themselves in the future. But they are not insurmountable.

Tech-enabled productivity tools have been transforming the nature of work at a torrid pace in the past two decades. Old skills were quickly replaced by new, and those who could not adapt became unproductive and irrelevant.

The COVID pandemic, in addition to wreaking havoc on businesses and jobs, has accelerated and fast-forwarded this trend of tech-enabled innovations at warp speed.

For example, consider the emergence of remote working, i.e., the work-from-home phenomena. Its widespread adoption happened almost overnight, and it now appears likely that working remotely will become a permanent fixture of how a significant slice of the population will work in the future. It is still too early to fathom the total impact of this, but an entirely new set of jobs, careers, and businesses will emerge to meet the demands of the new future of work.

You have a choice – change or become irrelevant.

Why is career reinvention so difficult?

The simple truth is that it is *perceived* to be hard because most people do not know how to go about changing careers. It is the do-not-know-how syndrome that deters people. Overcoming that is the most difficult part.

People are conditioned to operate within their skill sets and training, at jobs and within an industry where they feel comfortable. They feel secure in their comfort zone, and stepping outside that area is, well, uncomfortable. Hence, change is deemed hard.

Many also shy away from reinvention because they are afraid to fail. But this is a misplaced fear. Is anything worthwhile ever accomplished without taking risk? Doing nothing, in the face of stagnation or obsolescence, is insanity.

Reinvention is challenging to undertake when we are comfortable with a job and paycheck. We are lulled into a false sense of income security and may become lazy and procrastinate in dealing with the inevitable. It is only when we lose our jobs *and* get the proverbial kick-in-the-butt that we spring into action.

Rather than being reactive, become proactive in making the change.

For many, the fear of becoming irrelevant in the workplace may be their reason, their *Why*, for reinvention. For others, it may require deeper introspection to uncover their true *Why*.

The first step to reinventing yourself is finding the *Why*. After finding the *Why*, you have a binary decision to make. Commit to making a change and reinvent yourself or maintain the status quo. What are you going to do? If you commit to reinventing yourself, you have already taken the first step. You have discovered the *Why* you want to reinvent. The next steps are to determine the *When* and *What* of your reinvention.

The timing of *When* is the moment you commit yourself, and that time is now. Discovering your *What* is an exercise in finding clarity about what is most important to you, what matters most in your life, and what elements you want or do not want. Finding clarity is an iterative process of thinking and exploration. To engage in deep thought and introspection, you will need solitude and a distraction-free space to take a holistic view of your life. Rethink everything. I will help you establish criteria that must be present in your new job or career to ensure it will fulfill you, and your career path will emerge. It does, when people commit to it.

After the *Why, When,* and the *What*, the next step is *How* to reinvent. This requires developing a thoughtful, realistic plan. I have you take stock of your skills, resources, passions, and aspirations and map out the action steps you need to take to accomplish your *What*.

Finally, I show you how to *Execute* your plan. I guarantee that there will be challenges. Some things will go according to plan, but others will not. Remember, a plan is just that, a plan. It is not set in stone. You will learn how to pivot and change your execution methods as you encounter challenges.

If the plan does not work, change the plan, not the goal.

I recommend reading this book sequentially because each chapter is the next logical step after the preceding one. At the end of each chapter are *Key Takeaways* for action steps that you need to take. It is a good idea to make notes and refer to a preceding point to refresh your thinking as you progress on your journey to reinvention. Take the time to contemplate the *Key Takeaways*. In other words, do not rush the process.

Originally, I started writing this book because I too struggled with many of the same career challenges. But the arrival of the COVID pandemic, accelerating the disruption of jobs and people's lives, spurred the urgency of bringing this book to readers who may need help in reinventing themselves. Many old jobs have been lost, and many new ones are being created. I want to help you take advantage of these new career opportunities.

If you follow the guidelines in this book *and* put in the work – you *will* achieve success in reinventing yourself and your career. In the upcoming chapters, I show you the sequential steps, together with real-life anecdotes, on how to successfully reinvent your career.

Are you ready to take control of your future? Then, let us begin.

CHAPTER 1

A Reinvention Story:
When Failure Is Not an Option

Just after midnight on April 17, 1974, a 22-year-old man, nicknamed Bobby, boarded an Aeroflot flight in New Delhi, India, on his way to Copenhagen, Denmark, with a one-way ticket.

The young man was on a mission.

It was a mission to obtain higher education in Sweden, find a well-paying job, and make enough money to support his family back home – a mother, a young sister, and an ailing father. Bobby did not speak Swedish, was not enrolled in any university, did not have a job awaiting him, had no friends or support system, and did not know where he would live once he arrived. All he had was $200 and a dream. A dream and a determination to succeed.

Once airborne, Bobby could not sleep. How could he? This was a defining moment in his life. As the plane cruised through the night, Bobby looked out the window into the darkness and reflected on his life…

Bobby was born in New Delhi, India, and was raised in a middle-class family. A loving family where both parents doted on their children, Bobby and his younger sister Poonam, and ensured that their children received the best schooling possible. Bobby went to St. Columba's School, an all-boys Catholic school run by Irish missionaries. His sister went to the Convent of Jesus and Mary, an all-girls Catholic school, also run by missionaries. Both schools excelled in all-around academic education, where the English language was the natural medium of instruction. The schools served as great platforms for higher education at leading colleges, engineering institutes, and medical schools. After graduating from high school, Bobby studied at Delhi University and earned an undergraduate degree in economics and business management. He was 20 years old.

Soon after graduating from college, Bobby started looking for a career path. India, at the time, was still a poor, developing country with low wages. The opportunities for young college graduates to find a good starter job, such as a management trainee at a good company, depended more on who they knew rather than how qualified they were. Such trainee jobs were scarce, and after a year of trying, Bobby was unable to land a good job. In the meantime, his father's health was failing, and he was out of work. The family struggled with finances. As Bobby looked closely at the situation – unable to find a job with good prospects, an ailing father, and financial woes – he grew increasingly frustrated. When he saw many of his wealthy college friends traveling to the U.S., the U.K., and Canada for further education because their families could financially afford it, Bobby became even more frustrated and depressed at the prospect of not being able to make a meaningful life and support his family.

Providing for the family and building a better life for himself became a priority for Bobby. His mother said to him, "Bobby, you are our only hope." He knew the responsibility was now all his.

What was Bobby going to do?

He found a job with a local travel agency working as a tourist guide. His task was to accompany and guide hordes of foreign tourists on sight-seeing tours across India. This work was drudgery for him, and the meager wages he earned barely helped support Bobby and his family. This was not the life he had imagined or the career he wanted. He had grander visions.

He knew there was no real career or future for him in India. He had to leave and travel to the U.S. or Europe to continue with higher education, make good money, support his family, and build a better life for himself. But how? The family had no money to afford a college education for him in the U.S. There was not even money to buy an airline ticket. The future looked bleak, but Bobby continued to dwell on leaving India and frustratingly wondered how, how, how. He really, really wanted to go to the U.S., get an MBA degree, and find a good management job there. But the family financial constraints precluded this from becoming a viable option. He wondered if it were possible to work and attend college in the U.S. No, U.S. immigration laws were rigid, and it would be impossible for him to obtain a work visa that would allow him to work in order to support himself. Bobby began researching countries in Europe and discovered that Sweden allowed foreign workers to legally work there during the summer months, April to September. This was it, he thought. This was the solution. He could travel to Sweden, work all summer, save up enough money for the winter, enroll in a university, and earn an MBA. This was the break he needed. Yes, this was what he was going to do.

He told his parents about his plan to travel to Sweden. They were shocked and in total disbelief at the sheer audacity of it all. His mother thought it was a foolish idea and said, "You don't have a job lined up in Sweden, have no support system there, have no money, and you don't even speak the Swedish language. How can you possibly even think about this?" Bobby replied, "Mom, you told me that I was the family's only hope, right? Then have faith in me. I will make this happen."

Bobby borrowed money from an uncle to pay for the airline ticket and pocketed $200 for expenses. Sweden was an expensive place, and Bobby figured $200 would provide for about a week's worth of lodging, food, and travel. Once he arrived in Sweden, he would be racing against the clock to find a job. Any job would do.

As the airplane started its initial descent into Copenhagen's Kastrup Airport, Bobby's thoughts drifted...

He had taken a bold risk, a giant leap into the unknown where the outcomes had enormous consequences. He felt the excitement of the adventure but also great trepidation. He had a fleeting moment of doubt and thought, what if I fail? And then, he thought about his family, the circumstances that had brought him to take this colossal step, and he dismissed the notion of failure from his head. He felt his inner strength, his strong will, and sheer grit. He was prepared to do whatever it took to accomplish his mission. There was no turning back now. He was, literally, on a one-way ticket. Failure was not an option!

After arriving in Copenhagen and using his Fodor's Travel Guide, Bobby traveled by bus to the ferry station for the short crossing into Malmo, the third-largest city in Sweden, and continued by bus to nearby Lund University. He spent the entire day at the university campus looking around the beautiful medieval architecture, chatting in English with students and college counselors, looking at the job posting boards, and just enjoying the new experience and culture. Sleepless and physically exhausted, yet invigorated by this new and refreshing environment, he soaked in all that seemed so beautiful and promising – the promise of a new future.

As dusk began to fall, Bobby had a decision to make. Where was he going to sleep that night? While Lund University was a good place and nearby Malmo was a city where he might find work, he considered his best option to be to travel to either Stockholm or Gothenburg, the two largest cities in Sweden. Stockholm was the capital with a good university and the center of finance and industry, while Gothenburg was a large industrial city. Both had equally good prospects for finding menial jobs. At the bus station near Lund University, two buses were departing for overnight travel. One to Stockholm and the other to Gothenburg. Bobby flipped a coin, heads for Stockholm and tails for Gothenburg. Heads up, and he boarded the Stockholm-bound bus. Exhausted, he fell asleep almost immediately.

Upon arrival in Stockholm the next morning, he checked into a student hostel. After he washed up, Bobby went out on foot to explore the city. Stockholm was an incredibly beautiful city made up of several islands. It was extremely clean and organized, with virtually no signs of poverty, which was a far cry from India. The people were shy but polite and helpful. Bobby spent the next two days exploring the city, checking out the help wanted ads posted in supermarkets that were always in Swedish, a language he did not speak. He often asked people passing by to help translate the ads, but he had no success in finding work. That night at the hostel, he felt anxious. Almost three days in the new country with his $200 stash quickly depleting and no prospect of any work created a sense of panic. Bobby had befriended a Swedish student who was also staying at the hostel. He enlisted his help and combed through the help wanted ads in the local newspapers – dishwashers, waiters, garage attendants, security guards, and such. Because he did not speak the language, Bobby figured these jobs would be the easiest to get.

The following morning, Bobby's friend, the hostel mate, was kind enough to make a few phone calls responding to the ads. They found an eager employer. The manager of the cafeteria at an industrial plant on the outskirts of the city needed a dishwasher to work seven hours a day, Monday through Friday. He would pay a wage of SEK 15 per hour, which at the time was about $3 per hour. If Bobby was interested, he should show up at seven the next morning. Upon hearing this, Bobby jumped with joy. This was a breakthrough, he thought. This was the pathway to success.

The next morning, Bobby took a long bus ride and showed up for work. He had never washed dishes before, at least not on an industrial scale for the over 500 lunches served in the cafeteria. But he did it, with a smile on his face. This was one small step in building a new future. A week later, he found a second job working as a dishwasher at a nearby restaurant at night. Three weeks later, he found a third job as a busboy at another restaurant on weekends.

Life was getting better for Bobby, and the anxiety of running out of money began to lessen. He rented a room with a Swedish family and was working three jobs. Whatever he earned, he sent a third to his family back home, saved a third, and lived off the rest. He worked like this for six months and enrolled at Stockholm University for an intensive Swedish language course. Proficiency in reading, writing, and speaking the language was an obvious necessity for his post-graduate studies and his goal to land a good management job. He spent the next year going to school five days a week to learn Swedish. Fortunately, he extended his work permit without any difficulty and continued working two jobs – dishwashing at nights and busing tables on the weekends. As his language proficiency grew, Bobby upgraded his job and became a ticket booth attendant at the Stockholm subway system, where he worked nights and weekends. This job was perfect because it paid three times as much as the others and sitting in a quiet booth at night and on weekends gave him time to read and do his homework. Life was slowly getting better and progressing in the right direction.

A year later, Bobby was completely proficient in Swedish and began his MBA program at Stockholm University. He moved into the campus dorms and continued working at the subway at night and on weekends.

The MBA program was rigorous and demanding, yet Bobby remained focused on his eventual goal and continued to persevere. While his college mates partied and enjoyed campus life after classes, Bobby worked. He worked hard at his job and even harder at his studies with a determination to excel. He understood that his college friends would also be his competitors when the time came to find a good job. He knew that, as an immigrant, he had to stand head and shoulders above the crowds. Bobby's focus in his studies was finance. Given his economics degree, that was no surprise. He started to read voraciously. Over the following two years, he read every major book on finance, business management, and multinational corporations that he could get his hands on at the university library. And his efforts were about to pay off bigtime.

Close to his MBA graduation, in May 1978, the large corporate recruiters came calling at the campus, and Bobby started interviewing for jobs with several companies. There were a few jobs offers that he considered. Graduation day came, and Bobby made his choice. He accepted a job offer to work at the Stockholm office of PricewaterhouseCoopers (PWC).

That was a momentous day in Bobby's life – a joyously tearful one. Four years of hard, hard work, many sacrifices, and the bold risk of $200 and a dream had finally paid off in spades. And not one to rest on his laurels, Bobby set his sights on his next career goal.

He wanted to go to the United States of America. More specifically, he wanted to work in finance, on Wall Street.

Joining PWC was a strategic choice. It was a U.S. company headquartered in New York and provided a possible path for Bobby to go there. Over the next two years, Bobby worked harder and smarter than all his peers at PWC and received due recognition for his contributions. When he asked for a transfer to the Head Office in New York, it was promptly arranged. In 1980, Bobby went to New York City to work at PWC. He worked there for a few years and finally found his way into his dream career of trading interest rate derivatives on Wall Street.

By now, you have probably guessed that Bobby is the author of this book. I hope you find this biography inspiring and useful in your own journey of reinventing yourself.

I tell you this story because, while it may be fascinating to some, it is *not a unique story*. The reality is that each year thousands of immigrants embark on similar journeys to better their lives. And, they often succeed. I also tell this story in the hope that it inspires you in your own journey to reinvention. If a broke 22-year-old immigrant from India can make it with nothing more than determination and a dream...you can too!

Key Takeaways

1. We often surprise ourselves with how much courage, inner strength, will power, determination, and focus we can bring to solve a problem.

2. When your back is up against a wall and failure is not an option, muster courage and take bold risks.

3. Even though you may not have a fully baked plan, trust your intuition and go for it.

4. Determination and unwavering commitment to the goal are vital to overcoming the challenges that will come your way.

5. It is essential to adopt the right mindset, whatever it takes, to succeed in your own reinvention.

CHAPTER 2

Why Reinvent Yourself?

Why not?

Since you are reading this book, chances are that you are not entirely happy, satisfied, or fulfilled with your current occupation and are therefore contemplating a change. In the Introduction, I briefly touched on possible reasons for transitioning, but now, I want you to dive deeper and ask yourself some tough questions – similar to the soul-searching process Bobby went through in Chapter 1 – A Reinvention Story: When Failure Is Not an Option. By doing so, you will be on the path to discovering your true *Why*.

At this juncture of your reinvention process, I caution you not to get ahead of yourself by thinking about the obstacles or how you are going to remake yourself. Stay in the present moment and focus on just this one aspect – discovering your *Why*.

Ask yourself, do I *need* to reinvent myself and my career, or do I *want* to? There is a fundamental difference between these two reasons. The *need-based* change is often a forced change, such as when we are required to do something that we did not want to do voluntarily. The *want-based* change is of our own volition or desire to remake ourselves. But the two are not mutually exclusive, and frequently, the truth lies in the gray area between *need* and *want*.

A few common *need-based* reasons:

- Have you recently lost your job?
- Are you stuck in your career and feel it is going nowhere?
- Is your work environment so stressful that it makes you unhappy?
- Has your industry been adversely impacted by disruptive change?
- Do you fear stagnation and future job loss because your skills have become obsolete and irrelevant?

And a *want-based* reason:

- Have you perhaps discovered a new calling in life and want to pursue something completely different?

These are some of the most common and obvious reasons why people want to remake their careers. Your reason may be a combination of two or more of these, but the point is to look deep inside yourself to find your *Why*. Until you discover this, it will be difficult to find the *What*, so do not rush this process.

The real reason for wanting to change livelihoods is sometimes not obvious. Therefore, it is essential that *before* you embark on a career change, you discover, understand, and embrace the real motivation behind the contemplated reinvention. You must engage in self-reflection and some soul-searching to find out why you want to remake your career or reinvent yourself.

Take your time and think about this question deeply. Write a note to yourself – right now – to actively reflect on this because it is fundamental to the process of reinventing yourself.

For my latest reinvention, starting at age 60, it took me three months of intense and deliberate introspection and self-reflection before I found my true *Why* for reinventing myself, which I describe later in the book. I had recently encountered major setbacks in a short period of time and had to make some choices. And often, the offered options are never simple and easy, rather nuanced and contradictory. I had a choice to either maintain the status quo – live a life of relative material comfort but otherwise trapped in misery – or to start over. I focused and attempted to rethink everything in my life – the elements of my life that brought me joy and were important for me to retain, and those I wished to eliminate because they brought me pain. I also reimagined a more fulfilling life. What would a dream life look like? Many beautiful images of the 'dream life' emerged because I permitted myself to dream. And dream I did. And just as sure as when you wake up from a beautiful dream, the reality or practicality of fulfilling the dream hits you. What sacrifices and trade-offs would you have to make to chase that dream? Was the risk worth the potential reward? Was attainment of the dream even feasible? Tough questions, challenging reality. Yet, this soul-searching helped me find the answer.

The status quo was not acceptable. I did not want to just walk through life or retire. I wanted to feel alive and accomplish great things. I had a lot of life left in me. I had found my *Why* to reinvent.

Here is an exercise that you may find useful...

Find time for quiet solitude and do a deep dive within yourself. Take a holistic view of your life. That is, examine your life in its totality – your work, money, family, friends, hobbies, needs, wants, dreams, desires, passions, goals, and so forth. Include everything in this introspective process and ask yourself, what are the things that matter most? What elements do you want in your life, and just as importantly, what do you not? Both are critical to know. Remember, most people spend more time at work than with family and friends. Your work life is at the core of your personal universe and impacts everything else in your life and the choices you make.

But you must be truthful and honest with yourself.

This self-reflection will provide a good read on your personal compass and identify what you need to add, delete, or change to attain the life you desire and deserve. And if it includes reinventing your career, then you will know why.

Create a worksheet for your deep dive. In one column, list how you currently spend your time by including what you do. Complete this with as much detail as you possibly can – by day, week, and month. Include all the items you can think of, such as work, commuting, sleep, exercise, family time, hobbies, socializing, recreation, vacation, reading, and running errands. Leave nothing out. In the next column, list all the things you desire in your life – your aspirations – that you currently do not engage in. Now, reflect on the items in both columns and think deeply. Which ones, if any, do you want to eliminate or minimize? Which current items do you wish to have more of? And which of the aspirational elements must you have in your life?

An exercise like this presents us with a clear snapshot of where we are, where we aspire to be, and the gap between the two that needs to be bridged. Take your time doing this exercise.

The more work you put into the process,
the more likely you are to succeed.

Key Takeaways

1. Ask yourself *Why* you want to reinvent yourself? Do you *need* to or *want* to?

2. Do a deep dive within yourself to discover your true *Why*.

3. Alter your mindset – keep an open mind. Allow yourself to explore and pursue new ideas and how you think about them.

4. Give yourself permission to dream and reimagine your aspirational life.

5. Use the worksheet you created and ask yourself:

    •   What do you aspire to become?

    •   What kind of work would impassion you?

    •   What, if any, changes would you like to make to have a more fulfilling life?

    •   Do you have a desire to work for yourself or to become an entrepreneur?

CHAPTER 3

Impact of Technology and Exogenous Events

When contemplating reinventing our careers, one must consider and understand the macroeconomic backdrop of disruptive trends that are rapidly changing the global economy, the nature of business, the evolution of new skills, and the forces behind such changes that impact us. These are the forces that threaten to render our current skills obsolete and make our jobs and careers redundant.

Impact of technological innovation

In the past two decades, technology has transformed our world and lives and continues to do so at a frenetic pace. Those of us in midlife are keenly aware of how quickly things have changed – how we shop, how we socialize, how we communicate, how we work, and the very nature of our jobs and careers.

The emergence of the internet gave birth to the creation of whole new businesses and entirely new ways of doing things. Emailing, text messaging, and video conferencing have become the new staples of how we communicate. Social media platforms are a significant norm of how we socially interact. Online shopping, banking, learning, healthcare, travel and restaurant bookings, dating, and it seems that almost everything now gets done more efficiently online.

World-dominating companies have emerged to serve the needs of the new and ever-evolving internet economy, or e-commerce. Amazon, Apple, Facebook, Netflix, Google, Uber, and Airbnb, to mention just a few, are leading this tech-enabled evolution and have become some of the largest companies on the planet in less than two decades. They directly employ hundreds of thousands of people. Add to this list the software and hardware providers like Microsoft, SAP, Oracle, Adobe, Intel, Cisco, Nvidia, and other social media companies, and we have an echo system that employs millions of people with primarily tech-oriented skills.

All this was made possible solely by the creation of the internet. To say that the internet transformed the world and our jobs and careers is not an understatement.

Tech innovation, however, also has a dark side – the disruptive components. The adoption of new technologies has been upending the nature of work and businesses at a rapidly accelerating pace. Many old business models, jobs, and careers have either been rendered totally obsolete or marginalized by tech innovation. Consider how Amazon transformed the retail shopping industry. Uber disrupted the taxi and limousine sector, and Airbnb has done likewise to the hotel industry. Robot investment advisors and electronic trading platforms have replaced humans with machines in the financial services sector, and the list goes on.

Tech-enabled tools make the old ways of doing things redundant and inefficient, which renders previously valuable human skills obsolete. Many workplace tasks that were done by humans before, even highly skilled tasks, are now being automated. Machines are replacing humans. Numerous traditional jobs are becoming redundant, and many of the newly created jobs require different skills.

A report by the McKinsey Global Institute analyzing around 800 occupations in 46 countries, estimated that between 400 million and 800 million jobs could be lost due to robotic automation by 2030. That is a powerful and fast evolution of the future of work.

Impact of exogenous events

This evolution of technology impacting jobs and careers had already been accelerating at a rapid pace, and then, COVID happened.

Never in our lifetimes have we witnessed the speed and magnitude of devastation, disruption, and change in such a short time. As the virus pandemic seriously started to spread in the U.S. in early 2020, the government shut down the country with stay-at-home orders to prevent infected people from spreading the highly contagious killer virus. Except for a few essential services, all commerce and economic activity came to a sudden, screeching halt.

Offices, factories, schools, universities, restaurants, hotels, casinos, shopping malls, retail stores, sporting events, movie theaters, parks, beaches, beauty salons, barbershops, gyms, yoga studios, and tattoo parlors were shut down across most of the nation. The normal life that we had taken for granted was gone. Face-mask-wearing social distancing and work-from-home became the new normal.

It seemed that all this happened in a nanosecond. I am not sure if I had ever heard the term "social distancing" before the pandemic, and I had no idea that working from home was even a possibility for such a large slice of the working population.

Now, we know.

How disruptive has the impact of this pandemic been on our society and jobs? There is no word strong enough to articulate the mind-blowing jolt of this pandemic on our future lifestyles and livelihoods. Unprecedented. Unthinkable. Shocking. Take your pick.

At the time of going to press, millions of people in the U.S. had been infected by the virus, with tens of thousands of reported deaths. Millions had lost their jobs, and the official unemployment rate was in the double digits. The government responded quickly. It provided trillions of dollars in financial aid to individuals and businesses to support the unemployed and business owners, as they struggled to pay for expenses with no income coming in.

The loss of human lives and the enormity of the number of people infected is tragic. The mind-boggling number of people who lost their jobs so very quickly is absolutely devastating to those directly impacted. Combine this with the number of people already dissatisfied with their jobs, unemployed before the pandemic, and those being phased out due to technical advances, and you have a troubling employment market and frustration by many.

But all is not doom and gloom.

There is a big silver lining to this cloud if you choose to see it. These disruptive forces – tech innovation and exogenous events – have hastened the creation of new businesses, which in turn have begun to create new jobs, careers, and opportunities.

Consider the millions of office workers who now suddenly had to work from home. They needed secure internet connectivity and computing tools to connect with their office computer networks, teams, and customers. The demand for providers and enablers of home-based work setups soared almost overnight. Existing providers of these services saw their businesses booming, and many new business enterprises were started to meet the new demand for the services.

Take sanitizing services, for example. This is a big growth business sector now. Almost every workplace and public transportation system need to meet COVID-related sanitizing protocols as established by the CDC, on an ongoing basis. Again, existing providers of cleaning and sanitizing services saw booming demand for their services, and other new providers emerged to fulfill the soaring needs of this new market.

Other examples of new emerging career and business opportunities created by the pandemic resulted from fast-forwarding the demand for tech-based productivity tools like video conferencing (Zoom); enterprise communications systems (Slack); and cloud computing (Amazon Web Services, Microsoft, and Google). In turn, this set off the creation of an entirely new array of jobs and career opportunities.

When the country began to emerge from the lockdowns, we asked ourselves, what does the other side of the pandemic look like? It was impossible to answer this question with precision, given the uncertainties and unknowns. However, there was a high probability that life on the other side would be vastly different than before the pandemic hit us.

During the pandemic, there were mass behavioral changes, and a few of them were expected to be permanent. Some we could foresee, while others were yet to emerge. Many of these changes were of our own volition. But others were imposed upon us as new social norms, such as the regulatory rules established to ensure public safety and confidence.

Take social distancing, which is perhaps the single-most profound change that may become permanently embedded in our lives. It is the most important factor in how we live, interact with others, how and where we work, and how we operate our businesses. And, it has sweeping ramifications. Until such a time that an effective vaccine is developed to prevent infections from the COVID virus, this is deemed to be the only practical measure to ensure people from becoming infected. Most people understand the inconvenience of social distancing, yet they grudgingly accept and practice it for their own safety and the safety of others.

So, how does social distancing affect our lives?

While we were under stay-at-home orders, we pretty much stayed at home – cooking, cleaning, exercising, binge-watching movies on Netflix, or overworking, which led many people to reach the breaking point with their current position. When we ventured outdoors, it was perhaps to go for a walk where we instinctively maintained a healthy distance from other pedestrians. Or, we visited the supermarket wearing a face mask, trotting down one-way aisles as we shopped for items in an attempt to practice safe social distancing at all times. As lockdowns began to lift and we ventured back into the world, we thought about how we were going to conduct ourselves.

Will we continue to travel on crowded airplanes, trains, or buses without being assured of social distancing and a sanitized environment? The same goes for visits to the dentist, hair salons, gyms, restaurants, and the theater. Will there be multiple waves of the virus? How will those most vulnerable to becoming infected, the elderly and those with underlying medical conditions, protect themselves going forward? You get the point – almost every aspect of our lives will be viewed through the lens of caution. Social distancing is likely here to stay – in one form or another.

Impact on the future of work

To comply with the stay-at-home orders and ensure their workers' safety, many employers asked their employees to work from home, to the extent that they could, until the lockdowns were lifted.

And an amazing thing happened. People discovered that they could work effectively and efficiently from home. They plugged into their office's cloud-based computer networks. Using tech-enabled tools for emails, chats, and video conferencing, they could connect with their co-workers and teams, customers, and work tasks. The Zoom culture was born.

The productivity and prevalence of this rapid adoption to work from home took many by surprise. Enterprises large and small – banks, law firms, consultants, accountants, and even tech firms like Google, Facebook, Twitter, and Microsoft – conducted their businesses without missing a beat as many of their employees worked from home. Even TV and cable networks continued with their regular programming, showing their reporters and anchors working from home. This had never been experimented on at such a massive scale and proved to be immensely popular and very efficient.

Since this book is about reinventing your career, you are probably asking, "What's the impact of this historical narrative on *my job, my career*?" The answer is huge.

Consider the following example...

Imagine that you work in an office building in New York City and live in one of its suburbs. You wake up early, get dressed, and drive to the station to take the commuter train into the city. At the station, you have your temperature checked by an official and/or must show proof that you are free of the virus before you board the train, perhaps through an app on your smartphone. How comfortable are you being in a crowded train with hundreds of other people in close proximity?

When you arrive at the office building, you now go through the same process all over again before you can enter the elevator to your office on the 23rd floor. And then, you must wait in line for the elevator, and because of safe-social-distancing practices, they only allow three or four people on at a time. How do you feel about the delay? When you finally arrive on your floor, you may find that your office space, perhaps a cubicle in an open floor plan, is separated from your neighboring co-worker at a safe distance and enclosed in a plexiglass shield. Visits to the restrooms and the coffee room are restricted and perhaps monitored so that no social-distancing rules are violated.

What about the water-cooler chats with fellow workers? Forget it. How about lunch breaks? Step outside the building to get lunch, and you will encounter the same getting-into-the-office checkpoint routine that you went through in the morning. And during the commute home, you will endure the same discomfort and inconvenience as you did in the morning.

Now, let us be honest. How do you feel about your commute to and from the office at the end of the day?

Many employers will now ask or allow their office-based workers, a large portion of our workforce, to work from home or another remote location close to their homes because it will be more productive and less costly for both employees and employers. According to a recent survey conducted by Global Workplace Analytics, 30% of the respondents said they would continue to work from home even after the pandemic is over.

A few prominent tech companies like Twitter, Square, and Shopify told all their employees in May 2020 that they could continue to work from home permanently if they choose – a very thoughtful move to inspire employee morale and productivity, while at the same time reducing overhead expenses of office space. Many other tech and non-tech firms are seriously considering allowing a sizable portion of their total workforce to work from home.

But working from home will have serious ripple effects. Commuter train ridership will decline. In metro areas where restaurants, eateries, bars, and stores depend on a large portion of their business from neighboring office buildings, owners will undoubtedly see an adverse impact on their revenues since those customers will no longer come into town.

On the flip side, the providers of tech-based tools and solutions that enhance productivity and enable people to work remotely are likely to thrive from this acceleration of changing trends accidentally caused by this pandemic. Their prospects could not be rosier.

Remote working is the new future of work for a large segment of the labor force. And the enabling technologies – think video conferencing; cloud computing; artificial intelligence; robotics; 5G communications; work-from-home infrastructure; online health care, education, shopping, and entertainment; and other productivity-enhancing tools – are creating new career opportunities of the future.

Impact on the future of businesses

Each business, large or small, has been impacted. And, every company must re-examine and change its business model to stay relevant and profitable in the post-pandemic world.

Consider this...

Restaurants will have to reduce the number of seats to comply with the mandated social-distancing rules and add new sanitizing protocols to ensure the health and safety of its patrons and team members. Reducing the number of seats reduces revenues. Adding new cleaning and sanitizing protocols increases costs. This is a double whammy to a restaurant's profitability. The restaurant owner will have to figure out a way to be profitable or go out of business. Many industry experts predict that 25% or more of existing restaurants will be permanently shuttered.

Airlines. Can you contemplate getting on a crowded airplane, notwithstanding all the assurances and safeguards that may be put in place? With more adoption of video conferencing and less attendance at industry convention gatherings, business travel will decline. Personal travel will be adversely impacted, too. Airline operators will have to reduce capacity, the number of aircraft and flights, and comply with frequent airplane sanitizations, resulting in higher operating costs. Again, this amounts to less revenue, more expenses, and reduced or no profits. They will be laying off workers, thus becoming job destroyers and not job creators.

The commercial real estate landlords of office buildings, shopping malls, retail stores, and restaurants and the vendors who serve these industries are also impacted by the work-from-home phenomenon and closures of restaurants and stores. Reduced demand for office space and storefront properties will cause them to re-examine and modify their business models.

The same reasoning applies to an entire host of other businesses – hotels, sports stadiums, movie theaters, concert halls, gyms, and many more. All of them will have to re-examine their previous business models to see how they can tweak or completely reinvent their businesses to stay relevant and profitable in the post-pandemic world. For those who are unable, pulling down the shutters may be the only option.

And another group has yet to emerge – the entrepreneurs who discover and provide for the new opportunities created by the new paradigms of social distancing and remote working.

This is where I believe the biggest future career opportunities will emerge.

How do we prepare ourselves for the future?

We must have realistic optimism and do a lot of innovative thinking. We must throw out the old playbook, or at least the one that is now irrelevant.

With the right connectivity tools and infrastructure, remote workers will now be free to choose where they live since they do not have to commute to the office. A person working for an investment advisory company in New York will have the choice to live, for example, in Naples, Florida, in a community and climate more suitable to their lifestyle. I believe that remote working is here to stay for information and office workers who do not have to engage in manufacturing or face-to-face customer service. The technologies were already available to enable remote working. We are now beginning to witness the emergence of many new business startups gearing up to provide yet more tech-based tools to make remote working more efficient. Remote working empowers employees to seek career opportunities on a national or global scale without being confined to the vicinity of where they live. Likewise, companies will be able to tap into a larger pool of workers without geographic constraints – a win-win for all. Companies that are too rigid to change and adapt, meaning those that do not allow remote working for their employees, will be at a competitive disadvantage.

Where are the future jobs and career opportunities? They will be at the crossroads of technological innovation and remote working.

For those considering employment or entrepreneurship, think of transitioning into future tech sectors – productivity-enhancing software; computing hardware; data sciences and analytics; artificial intelligence; robotics; logistics; 5G telecommunications; cloud computing; and fintech. That is where future economic growth and exciting career opportunities are likely to be found.

For those inclined toward self-employment as an independent professional, the world of opportunities is wide open. Again, digitization and tech-enabled tools make such a career transition possible. Consider trending growth sectors. Many new opportunities will emerge in the delivery of online learning and education; health care; productivity-enhancing tools; professional services like coaching, content creation, and marketing; financial services; and the list goes on – limited only by our ability to think creatively.

Exogenous events, like the COVID pandemic, serve to accelerate the prevailing trends of tech innovation, and this pandemic became the catalyst for turbo-charging the pace of disruptive change.

With the loss of jobs and obsolescence of skills, it is no surprise that many people are feeling anxious about their futures and do not know what to do or where to turn for help.

This is understandable because the job market we once knew is evolving quickly and drastically.

To thrive, not just survive, in the future where rapid creative disruption renders many skills, jobs, and careers obsolete, we must prepare to change ourselves – our mindset, our skills, our needs, and our wants.

Rethink everything. Reimagine your new life. Rediscover your passions. Reinvent your career.

Key Takeaways

1. Understand the impact of technological innovation and exogenous events on skills, jobs, and careers.

2. Change and creative disruption forces will continue to evolve the nature of work. Old ways of doing things will be replaced by new ways at an increasingly rapid pace. Consequently, we must continue to upgrade our learning and skills to take advantage of the new opportunities that emerge.

3. Rethink everything. By everything, I mean EVERYTHING! How you live, what is enormously important to you, what elements you want in your life, how you interact with others, how and where you work, what you want from your career, how you provide and care for your family, your work-life balance, and your health.

CHAPTER 4

When to Reinvent Yourself?

There has never been a more opportune time to reinvent your career than the present – the moment is *now*. There is no utility in waiting for the perfect time because there is no such thing. Conditions are never ideal. And, we rarely ever have complete information or know with certainty what the eventual outcomes will be. Most decisions that we make, in life and business, are made under conditions of uncertainty. Some good choices may result in bad outcomes, while some poor decisions may result in good results. Yet, we must decide and act.

Inaction is a losing proposition.

So, when is it time to reinvent?

During chaos and disruption

Chaos and disruption often create more opportunities than we realize – if we choose to see them. And, it is a great time to consider reinventing ourselves.

According to this CNBC report from April 14, 2020…

"Last summer Jon Poteet fulfilled a dream when he opened Shine Distillery & Grill a 260-seat restaurant and micro-distillery in Portland, Oregon's historic Williams district. These days, however, rather than serving up regional cuisine and signature cocktails to a packed house, Poteet and his 25-person staff are doing a brisk business in private-label hand sanitizer.

"Welcome to the coronavirus economy. Many small- and mid-sized businesses are hanging on by a thread as demand dries up and authorities in many parts of the country order nonessential establishments to close their doors temporarily. But some entrepreneurs and nonprofits are retooling in an effort to survive — and/or make a difference — by meeting the demand for hand sanitizer, face masks and other products in short supply.

"Poteet saw his restaurant business begin to slow in early March, when the first reported cases of COVID-19 infection in the Seattle area stoked fears about dining out. In mid-March, Oregon Gov. Kate Brown ordered the state's bars and restaurants to stop all on-site dining and limit sales to takeout and delivery. Fortunately for Poteet, Shine had already begun making, selling and donating hand sanitizer even before the order brought Portland's booming restaurant scene to a near standstill.

"Eighty percent alcohol by volume, Shine's hand sanitizer sells for $1 per ounce and is made from alcohol typically used to produce vodka and other spirits, along with a commonly used food additive for thickening. The Centers for Disease Control and Prevention recommends

using hand sanitizer with at least 60% alcohol, although vigorous handwashing is preferable. Shine's hand sanitizer is produced on site. Shine's distiller, Shannon Mosley, came up with the formula by tweaking a recipe found online.

"'Our business doubled overnight. We had two lines out the door, one for seating in our restaurant and the other for hand sanitizer. I realized that this was a game changer,' says Poteet, reflecting on the changes that took place right after his hand sanitizer venture started to attract media attention.

"In recent weeks, Poteet and his staff have been fielding hundreds of calls a day from anxious consumers wanting hand sanitizer, people seeking donations of it, media outlets, and other distilleries interested in making it. Poteet estimates that he's given Shine's recipe for hand sanitizer to some 300 distilleries across the country.

"'I'm a believer in wanting a healthy community. Giving back to the community will always pay off,' says Poteet, who has also given away thousands of bottles of Shine's hand sanitizer to individuals and community organizations.

"'Anybody who walks in the door gets three ounces, whether they ask for it or not,' he notes.

"Since early March, Shine has sold more than 4,000 bottles of its hand sanitizer, ranging in size from 6 oz to 16 oz. On any given day, the business generates almost

as much revenue as it brought in prior to the temporary
suspension of its sit-down restaurant business, accord-
ing to Poteet. That's about $6,000 a day."

This story is a great illustration of how an entrepreneur
saw and seized an opportunity for reinvention arising from
a crisis.

When you lose a job

This change is forced upon you, and it is an opportune time
to engage in deliberative thought about your next position or
career path. In these instances, you probably have no choice
but to seek another livelihood.

It is in situations like these, when people lose their jobs,
that most career transformations occur. There is plenty anecdotal evidence for this. I am sure you know of someone who
was fired from a job and went on to blaze an entirely new
career. While losing a job is no fun, it has its upsides. For
example, it frees your mind from the attachments and obli-
gations associated with your previous role and forces you to
rethink your future. This is a great time to consider making a
career change instead of merely finding another job unless, of
course, you need an immediate paycheck.

A friend of mine had just turned 50 when he was laid off
from his job, due to cost-cutting, at a prestigious Wall Street
investment banking firm where he had worked for 20 years.
He was devasted when he received the news. He had worked
hard throughout his entire career – long hours including
weekends – as a high-yield credit analyst and had made a successful career earning a high six-figure income each year. He
had built his entire lifestyle wrapped around his job. It defined

him. Losing it was a crushing blow to his well-being. What was he going to do now?

He was fortunate and had accumulated substantial savings over the years, so he did not feel immediate pressure to go out and search for another job. He took some time off to figure out what he wanted to do next. He started to think, reflect, and discovered a few things. He felt burnt out by the high stress of working on Wall Street and did not want to do that anymore. He also knew that he wanted to accomplish greater career success – he was not the retiring kind of man and had many productive years left in him. So, his mind turned toward doing something more meaningful, something entrepreneurial. He assessed his core skills of deep experience in finance and capital markets and wondered how he could apply those in the future. Four months into this mode of self-reflection, he came upon the idea of reinventing his career. He wanted to work as the finance chief at a smaller entrepreneurial company. He tapped into a network of recruitment firms and started his job search.

Almost a year later, he found his dream job as the Chief Financial Officer (CFO) at a startup software company that was developing a platform for enabling and processing online commerce payments. That was three years ago. He is now happier than ever and accomplishing some extraordinary things in his newly found career.

When your career is in a rut

It is not uncommon that many people, notwithstanding how successful they may have been, find their careers in a rut. They feel stuck and that their career is going nowhere. There seems to be limited or no potential for personal growth and not much new learning or promotion to assume a greater role. Such a situation is best described as a state of drudgery – where you wake up in the morning and drag yourself to work simply to earn the paycheck. There is not much joy or sense of fulfillment.

Here is my litmus test for determining if your career is in a rut: If you don't feel like you are chomping at the bit, full of joy and excitement, about getting to work each morning or if you are not constantly thinking about how you can become more creative, effective, and contribute more, then your career is, dare I say it, in a rut.

When you see these symptoms of being in a rut, it is time to consider making a change. The easier option is to maintain the status quo because it is the 'comfort' zone of the known dissatisfactions that entrap us. The courageous action is for you to take control of the situation and do something about it.

When you discover a new calling in life

This is easier since you already know, in some meaningful way, your reason *Why* you want to shift careers. Perhaps, it is a dream or passion whose time has come, and you wish to embark on a more fulfilling journey.

Greg Mikusinski was a realtor in Miami, Florida. One of many thousands of realtors in the area peddling condo sales and apartment rentals to snowbirds and foreigners seeking a place to live in the sunny paradise. He eked out a meager living to pay his bills, but his heart was not in this line of work.

When I first met Greg, I liked him instantly. He reminded me of a younger version of myself. At that time, Greg was in his mid-thirties. Tall, charming, and with a delightful edge of hustle in his personality. He loved the good life – good food, wine, people, and boats. Yes, boats. That was his real passion.

Especially, the big mega yachts. He dreamed and dreamed about one day owning a big boat or two.

Greg's life revolved around the boating scene in Miami. He could be found at every boat show and marina in the city, where he befriended yacht brokers, yacht crews, and the staff of the big yachts. He spent time hanging around them. Greg had an entrepreneurial streak but did not quite know what to do with his life or career. We often spent time together, and I mentored him with some tough, big-brotherly love to help him get his career moving down a more meaningful path. Since boats were his passion, I encouraged him to explore a career or business related to the boating world.

And then, an opportunity presented itself to Greg. A friend of his, John, was the chef on one of the mega yachts docked in Miami. These yachts regularly need provisions – high-end foods, wines, and liquors to cater to the owner's guests and parties aboard the yacht. John offered Greg the opportunity to find and provide about $25,000 worth of provisions. Greg had no idea or experience of how do to this but readily accepted the offer – and delivered the goods.

That was the start of his Provide & Supply business and company. Five years later, Greg's company provisions over 100 mega yachts around the world, and he has built a highly profitable seven-figure business. He now lives in Spain, is happily married with two children, and has two boats of his own.

A great story of reinventing one's career around a passion – his passion for boats.

When your skills become obsolete

This is when technological innovation makes certain skilled workers redundant. This is another and more insidious kind of change that forces you to reinvent yourself and your career. Productivity is constantly going up. Many jobs are disappearing, while new ones are being created. As described earlier, this creative disruption is here to stay and will continue to evolve the nature of jobs. If you recognize that your skills are becoming irrelevant or fear that they will in the future, it is time to consider upgrading your skills or reinventing yourself into an entirely new career.

Over two decades ago, most listed securities trading occurred on exchanges, such as the New York Stock Exchange (NYSE), the Chicago Mercantile Exchange (CME), the Chicago Board of Trade (CBOT), and other major exchanges, where human floor traders executed securities transactions. Today, almost all trading is done on electronic platforms. Tens of thousands of those floor traders lost their jobs over the years because the adoption of new technologies rendered their skills obsolete.

Tech-enabled marketplace platforms have eliminated the middleman in many sectors. Think about how the direct-to-consumer sales of goods have taken away business from wholesalers and retail outlets of consumer products and services – apparel, consumables, personal insurance, and so forth. Similarly, direct business-to-business marketplaces, or electronic platforms, have either wholly eliminated the need for intermediaries or taken a large chunk of business away from them. Again, technology has rendered obsolete the skills and jobs of many people.

When you see secular trends that begin to adversely affect your industry, company, or business, it is time to reevaluate your career prospects and take action to reinvent your career.

These disruptive trends are increasing the urgency for people to become more proactive in adapting to new trends and making the appropriate shifts in upgrading their skills and/or their careers.

Key Takeaways

1. It is time to reinvent yourself when you lose your job; your career is in a rut; disruptive forces adversely impact your skills or relevance; or you have found a new calling in life.

2. Do not procrastinate the decision. There is no such thing as the perfect time, so do not wait.

3. Commit to remaking your career. Commitment is strongest when you have the motivation and will-power to embark on this journey of reinvention. It requires relentless perseverance. Write your commitment on paper, your computer, or your smartphone where you are reminded of it daily.

4. Find an accountability partner, a spouse, a friend, or someone close and encourage them to push and support you in your endeavor. There will be challenges during this journey, and to come out successfully on the other side, you must stay committed. This is critical.

CHAPTER 5

Reinvent to *What*?

Now that you know your *Why* and have committed to remaking your career, the next question is: Reinvent to *What*?

For a few, the answer may be readily apparent, but for most, it will likely become clear only through a process of discovery. You may have some vague idea of what you would like your next career path to be but are not quite sure or are considering multiple paths. This is a natural state of mind and requires a substantial amount of iterative thinking and exploration. Again, do not rush the process. These insights may take time to form.

Figuring out your future career path is tough but not insurmountable. The process is challenging and can feel overwhelming, but it is of critical importance to your life and requires deep deliberative thinking. There will be moments of despair, but do not let them get you down.

Do not be disheartened and give up. Stay the course.

Let me share a personal story about how I found clarity when I reinvented my latest career. I hope it inspires you.

While my circumstances and story will not be the same as yours, the underlying thought principles and action steps identified here will serve as a useful guide in your journey.

When lightning strikes

For over 25 years, I was a professional trader on Wall Street. I traded interest rate derivatives and loved it. The markets, taking and managing risk, the intellectual challenge of creating novel trading strategies, and the adrenaline rush of trading fit my DNA like no other. Trading was my calling in life, my purpose, and the ideal career for me. And a successful one at that. Over the span of two decades, I worked as a trader at world-class institutions like Chase Bank, Chemical Bank, a hedge fund, JPMorgan Chase, and Cantor Fitzgerald.

I enjoyed what I did for a living, and the financial rewards provided for a comfortable, upscale lifestyle – a beautiful home in Princeton, New Jersey, two country club memberships, three Porsches in the garage, a German Shepherd dog, nice vacations, plenty of friends, and a small, happy family. The American dream had come true for this poor immigrant from India. Life was good!

Then, 2008 happened.

The financial crisis, led by the meltdown in the U.S. housing market, hit the economy hard, many prominent financial institutions failed, and others were rescued by the U.S. government. And, we found ourselves in the Great Recession. The U.S. central bank (the Fed) eased its benchmark interest rate to zero and pumped several trillion dollars into the banking system to dig the economy out of this calamitous hole.

The Fed's move, lowering rates to zero, was the death knell for my trading business. With interest rates pegged at zero, market volatility, which is the up and down movement on any given day, began to decline. As a result, trading volumes of derivatives started to decrease and, along with it, my income from trading profits and commissions. This decline in bond trading and related derivatives continued through 2010. At that time, it became apparent to market participants that the economic recovery and, more specifically, bond and derivative trading volumes were not likely to return to normal for several years.

I was working at Cantor Fitzgerald at that time, where I essentially ran my own business – trading and selling interest rate derivatives – under the umbrella of the company. Profits were split 70/30, meaning I took home 70% of the profits and commissions, and the company received 30%. This was a good setup. Eat what you kill. But now, I began to seriously ponder the prospects of my business if this condition of zero rates were to persist, a highly probable outcome, for an extended period. What would happen to my livelihood?

A sense of frustration, and even despair, began to overwhelm me. I had not yet attained financial independence to the extent that I did not have to work for a living. The writing was clearly written on the wall – this part of my career would soon be over, and I needed to find another way of making a living. What the next thing was, I did not know. And I struggled to come up with realistic ideas. There were moments of doubt, where I panicked at the thought that this may be the end of the line. How was I going to make a living?

I did not have to wait too long to find out because other unrelated, unexpected, and sudden events threw me into the middle of a Perfect Storm. In September 2010, I had major spine surgery and was out of commission from work for a couple of months. In November of that year, I attempted to go back to work, commuting by train from Princeton to New York as I had done the past 15 years. I discovered that I was unable to perform at my best, given the debilitating back pain that resulted from the physical strain of commuting and being on the trading floor for nine hours a day. So, I quit my job. Soon after, my marriage of 25 years broke up.

It felt like being struck by not one, nor two, but three bolts of lightning. In a span of three months, my life, as I knew it, had just blown up. Big time!

What was I going to do now?

Dealing with just any one of the three hits – major spine surgery, job loss, broken marriage – at any time is tough. Attempting to deal with all three at the same time seemed like a Herculean task for me.

I spent the next two months healing from my surgery and contemplating what to do next. I was almost 60 years old. I was hit hard emotionally by the marriage break up and was unsure about what to do next with my career. There were no ready answers. Going from life was good to life was shit, to put it mildly, was an unthinkable disaster. For me, the hardest part was the emotional pain from the marriage breaking up. We had a wonderful son, Kabir, who was 21 at the time and in college in New York. The prospect of the family breaking up was painfully gut-wrenching. I was still living in my Princeton home at the time and struggled daily with my emotions and the question – what was I going to do now? The choices were either to stay and maintain the status quo or move on. I struggled with that decision, a lot.

However, even in an emotionally wrecked and physically distraught state, it was apparent that I had to do something. I did not quite know what that 'something' was, but I knew that doing nothing was not an option. I had dreams of living a fulfilling life. I wanted to accomplish more great things in my career because I had a lot of life ahead of me. I had to take steps to right my ship. And then, that 'something' began to emerge.

I committed to reinventing myself. I took bold and courageous action to deal with all three events simultaneously by giving myself the opportunity to think and figure out what I wanted in my life and what I wanted to do next professionally.

Taking action

It was clear to me that the first thing I needed to do was to stabilize myself, both emotionally and physically. I took stock of the resources available to me. I had some savings and passive income. If I could simplify my future lifestyle and rein in expenses, I could survive financially for a couple of years until I found my next career path. Not everyone is as fortunate. If that is the case for you, find a job to earn some income to support you through this transitional period.

But I also wanted a fresh start. I wanted to reevaluate everything in my life. I needed a refreshing space to think and an environment that would be most supportive of this new journey I was about to undertake. It was a bold move to make at age 60 and fraught with risks. But I dug deep and drew on inner strengths and a similar experience from earlier in my life to muster the courage to change. The status quo was not an option.

In early 2011, I left my home in Princeton and moved to Miami to restart my life with a clean slate. It was emotionally hard, extremely hard – perhaps the most emotionally difficult period of my life. Now, I was on my own, alone and without the support system that I had grown to have great comfort in. Alone in a city new to me where I knew no one and without a sustainable livelihood. The first few months were very difficult, where I was just trying to regain my emotional stability, and there were many nights when I cried. Yes, grown men also cry. There were several moments of doubt where I wondered if I had made the right decisions, but I persevered through the pain.

Restarting afresh meant first laying a foundation upon which I could build a meaningful life and career. I began to simplify my life. I now lived in a small yet comfortable apartment near the beach. I gave up my country club memberships, quit my hobby of racing Porsches, and eliminated most other discretionary expenses, such as expensive wines and vacations. I also embarked on a disciplined regimen of physical therapy, exercise, and yoga to strengthen my spine and get physically fit.

---

*The new personal finance mantra was
to spend on needs and not wants.*

Attempting to rebuild a life at age 60 – alone in a new city where I did not know anyone, had no friends or network, while still under the immense emotional stress – is no easy task. As you can imagine, I had constant stress and anxiety considering the many unknowns. Obviously, there were numerous moments of doubt – whether I had chosen the right path or made the right decisions. Each time I grappled with uncertainty, I checked my personal compass to ensure that it was still showing true north. If not, I pivoted to stay on course.

Immediately after moving to Miami, I became reclusive and did not maintain contact with friends and former business acquaintances. Partly because of my distressed emotional state, I was reluctant to engage in conversations or socially interact with them. Over time, I realized this was a mistake, and I corrected it by reconnecting with friends who had been supportive in the past.

The quest for what to do next, career-wise, had become a 24/7 obsession for me. It was always in focus, at the forefront of my mind. I did not know precisely what I wanted to do occupationally. But I did know that whatever my new gig was going to be, it must have three essential components – it had to be intellectually stimulating, something I would be impassioned with, and had to provide a certain level of income. I also knew that I did not want to work for a large corporation anymore. With those basic criteria, the choice of paths emerging was either taking the entrepreneurial route or finding a great job with a smaller firm.

I listed and assessed my skill set. I was a derivatives trader and a pretty darn good one at that. I knew the markets, had expert skills in managing market risk in investment portfolios, and was a strategic thinker and creator of complex, structured trading ideas. I had management experience across multiple industry sectors, had entrepreneurial experience from having co-founded two startup businesses, and was multicultural and multilingual, with a broad and in-depth knowledge of global economics, business, and finance, having lived and worked on three continents. While these skills might appear impressive, they are, unfortunately, not unique. And the reality of the employment marketplace is – regardless of my abilities and how smart or experienced I thought I was – few would hire a 60-year-old man.

After eliminating seeking a job at a smaller firm, the entrepreneurial path was emerging as the only viable option. I began to explore the landscape for entrepreneurial opportunities and toyed with a few interesting ideas, the most promising of which was sticking to my financial experience.

How about starting my own hedge fund?

Given that some of my core skills were about in-depth knowledge of the bond markets and derivatives and that I loved to trade and was good at managing market risk, the prospect of becoming my own boss and making tons of dough as a hedge fund manager was alluring. It was a seemingly logical next step toward a career based on my prior experience.

There was one catch, though. A big one. Would I be able to raise a critical amount of capital to start a fund?

The hedge fund industry had evolved rapidly and become institutionalized. It no longer sufficed to raise a couple of million dollars from friends and family and bootstrap a new fund. One had to get a large chunk of institutional money, from pension funds, endowments, or other funds who seed startup hedge funds. Without institutional investor backing, the fund would have little potential to grow or create enough profits to sustain the costs of operating the business. To get institutional money, a hedge fund manager must demonstrate a formal, documented track record of trading profitability over several years.

I lacked that formal documentation. Although I knew I was a good trader, could make money under most market conditions, and had that reputation among clients I had worked with previously, I knew it would be tough to raise money without a documented paper trail. This was the only significant obstacle I had to overcome to launch the fund. This was the problem with working as a trader at a big bank. My profit and loss statements belonged to the bank, and I could not take that performance record with me to share with the outside world. I could not capitalize on my previous success under their employment.

From the onset, the odds were stacked against me. But I also knew that success would be huge if I could land even just one institutional client. I had a business plan and pitched and persevered over the next couple of years to raise capital. A few high net-worth individuals in my network offered to invest modest amounts of money in the fund, but it was not enough. I was unable to convince a single institutional investor to write a big check.

I had tried my best to raise capital from an institutional investor to start the fund but failed. The reality of the market-place dynamics sunk in, and I decided not to waste any more time and resources on this venture. And then I asked myself, what's next?

The road trip

It was now July 2015, over four years since I left Princeton, and I found myself at the crossroads of life – again. I was now 64 years old, although a young 64. My spine had healed, and I was in good physical shape. But that big question still loomed large, what should I do with my career?

I needed a break. A vacation, perhaps. Solitude. Some time to think.

And then, an idea dawned on me. Why not a road trip? A long, cross-country road trip. This was a bucket-list item for me, and now was perhaps the best time to do it.

I love to drive. Driving a well-tuned sports car is relaxing therapy for me. Before my life unraveled in late 2010, I used to race Porsches as a hobby at various racetracks around the country and still owned two of them. Spontaneously, I decided to do it.

This road trip was inspired by a quest for discovery, on many levels – discovery of self in a spiritual sense, discovery of hopefully a big new perspective on life, and discovery of my own endurance. I wanted solitude, so this was a solo journey. There were no specific itineraries nor any planned destinations to visit, other than knowing that I wanted to drive the roads less traveled and be with nature – mountains, forests, rivers, lakes, and coastlines – and visit the upper Midwest and Western parts of the country. And, there was no timeline to complete the trip. This journey was guided simply by whim, of driving wherever and whenever. The only rules I set for myself were to drive mostly during the daylight hours and totally disconnect from the world – no emails, no texting, and no incoming phone calls. The only usage of my iPhone was for navigation, taking pictures, or an emergency call if needed.

Then, there was the choice of which car to take for this trip. I had two vehicles at the time – a silver Porsche 911 Turbo S and an orange Porsche 911 GT3RS. The Turbo S was loaded with creature comforts and better suited for long-distance driving. The GT3RS was set up for the track. It was a harsher ride with racing seats, sparse comforts, and seemingly not appropriate for such a long road trip. But the car was more fun, loud, and a precise handling machine that after eight years of ownership still got my adrenalin going each time I sat behind the wheel. We had a long bonding history with over a hundred track days together, where we experienced exhilarating thrills and several moments of near-fatal disasters while racing. This car had become a part of my soul. And since this trip was largely a journey of the soul, it was a no-brainer to do it with my 'soulmate' and find the limits of our collective endurance.

The car was a two-seater stick shift with a roll cage behind the seats without much room for luggage or supplies. I packed a few tools and spares in the little trunk and jammed an overnight clothes bag, some protein bars, and water in the passenger seat.

So, on a hot day in July 2015, I drove the car out of the garage and began an epic 9,000-mile journey and found a new career.

This is how it happened…

Drove from Miami to Montana; Oregon; down the Pacific coastline to California; through Death Valley; Nevada; Arizona; Utah; Colorado; New Mexico; Texas; and back to Miami. I visited a few spectacular national parks like Yellowstone, Yosemite, Grand Canyon, and Zion.

The first couple of days of driving were about covering some ground to get to the mountain states, and my brain was still half stressed and stuck. It was perhaps after day 3 that I started to decompress. By the time I reached Montana and those beautiful mountain roads, I was in a state of nirvana. By day 8, it took effort to remember which day of the week it was.

There was no defined schedule other than waking up each morning and just 'feeling' where I wanted to drive. But there was one constant – I always sought the less-traveled roads. At sundown, I would find lodging in the closest town. Sometimes, I stayed in a luxury hotel, but other times, it would be a roach motel. At times, I had gourmet meals, but I also had roadside burgers to go. There were many memorable places and among my favorites in terms of natural beauty: Montana, Oregon, the Pacific coastline, Death Valley, Arizona, Utah, and Colorado. Red Lodge, Montana and Durango, Colorado are two very cool towns to visit.

The solitude of driving six to ten hours a day on uncrowded and desolate roads, often through spectacularly beautiful scenery, totally disconnected from the world, listening to the never-tiring roaring sound of the powerful engine behind me, led to a lot of reflection, thinking, and perspective gathering. Communing with nature, and the ever-changing landscape, began to filter the noise out of my life. It was becoming a lot clearer and obvious what I wanted in my life and what I did not – what was enormously important and mattered the most.

On day 12, as I drove through Zion National Park in Utah and onto Route 12, I had my Eureka moment.

As I drove and reflected on my life, I thought about the different jobs, places, people, and experiences that had impacted my life in meaningful ways. And one thing stood out – people – those who had been a positive force in my life, who had helped and mentored me. I thought about the people who I, in turn, had helped, mentored, and advised over the years. And just like clouds that part to let the sunshine in, the idea of my next career began to emerge. How about becoming a coach? A coach to business leaders. I had always enjoyed and sought the company of smart, bright people to learn from and exchange ideas. Coaching could be a mutually rewarding learning experience where I could mentor, advise, and help others, and they could be a source of new learning for me. Intellectually engaging, yes. Passionate about this, absolutely. Will it provide adequate income? Realistically, yes. And I would not work for a large corporation. Becoming a coach fulfilled all my criteria. Yes, this was it. Coaching was going to be my new career!

Over the next three days as I drove home to Miami, I thought more about this and made mental notes about what I needed to do in terms of further research, exploration, and planning to get this going.

When I arrived home and had gotten some sleep, I went all-in to making this new career a reality.

Key Takeaways

1. Finding clarity about a new career path is an iterative process of thinking and exploration. It may be tough but stay committed.

2. Clarity is the foundational blueprint for the next steps to reinventing your career.

3. To accomplish deep thinking and exploration, it is essential to create a space for reflection. I highly recommend a period of solitude, disconnecting from the day-to-day distractions and stresses to separate the noise from what is important in your thinking.

4. Look back into your own life and reflect on how you have dealt with challenging situations in the past – what worked and what did not and how you best think and explore. Draw on those insights and inspire yourself to find clarity.

5. Identify and list your skills and resources. Write them down.

6. Articulate the essential elements that are important to you and the criteria that must be present in the new career. Again, write these down.

CHAPTER 6

How to Plan a Reinvention

Now that you have figured your *Why, When,* and *What,* the next step is *How* to plan a career reinvention.

The first step in this part of the journey is to develop a plan. Planning is essential since it provides a roadmap for the journey you are about to undertake. Proper planning keeps you focused and helps you navigate the road, or roads, to your ultimate destination.

Imagine that you are about to embark on a road trip from city X to city Y. X is where you are today, and Y represents your desired destination. How would you plan and prepare for this trip before you hit the road? Chances are that your planning would include at least the following:

- Map the route you are going to drive.
- Plan for fuel, rest, and meal stops.
- Make lodging reservations en route, if the trip requires an overnight stay.
- Pack appropriate clothing and supplies.
- Ensure that the car is roadworthy and fueled up.
- Check traffic and weather conditions.

This thoughtful preparation is essential to ensure that you arrive safely and without hassle. Similarly, you need to develop a plan for the journey to your new career.

Start with research

Research is the gathering of information and knowledge. We want to gather all the relevant information that we are likely to need for developing an effective action plan. This step applies whether you are seeking employment; launching out on your own as an independent consultant, freelancer, or other professional; or starting a business or partnering in one.

The researched information not only guides you in developing a step-by-step roadmap for your journey but will also either affirm the thesis of your *What* or uncover some hard facts that refute it. How much research should you do? Only do as much as you deem adequate to make decisions with confidence. Avoid the temptation of digging deeper and deeper into a rabbit hole and becoming caught in never-ending searches. But also ensure that you have done enough research to make an informed decision. Your goal should be to find information that will either confirm or refute your thesis, not just support your current goals.

What type of information are you seeking? Start by looking for information that provides a macro overview of the industry sector or profession you are targeting.

For example…

- **Growth trends:** Is the industry or profession growing or expected to grow in demand, or is the industry in decline?
- **Market size:** Research the dollar sales, number of providers, and number of people employed in your targeted industry.

- **Industry participants:** Who are the dominant companies and agencies operating in the sector?

- **Regulatory, licensing, and professional organizations:** Who and what are the respective roles of various industry or professional organizations in the sector?

- **Compensation:** What is the data on salaries for professionals in the industry?

- **Location:** Should you relocate based on the geographic and demographic information?

- **Hiring protocol:** How are people hired? Is it through recruitment firms and websites that specialize in recruiting talent for the industry? How do you get in touch with them?

- **Other relevant information:** What is unique to this industry? Do you have a value add?

Where do you find this information? Google is an excellent initial place to start. Trade organizations are another good resource for more specialized and detailed information. And if you know people in your network who are already in the industry or profession, then seek them out and learn firsthand about their insights and experience.

The purpose of obtaining this macro overview is twofold...

1. It will **validate your premise** and enable you to further drill down the information funnel and help you develop a plan for specific actions. This is a critical point in the reinvention process, and you must be certain that the chosen career path fulfills your criteria for change as set out under Chapter 5, Key Takeaway 6.

After analyzing the research, it is vital that you feel confident in the attainment of your envisioned career change. While the envisioned career change is expected to be challenging, it must nevertheless be realistic. That is, it should be feasible and not just a wishful-thinking pie-in-the-sky dream. For example, if you are currently a 50-year-old financial advisor and dream of becoming an astronaut – is that realistic, really? My advice would be to enjoy the dream but keep your day job.

OR

2. The research findings may **invalidate your thesis** for the envisioned career change. The key is that this happens early in the research stage. That is a good thing because you can quickly self-adjust and go back to the preceding step, Chapter 5 – Reinvent to *What*?, and start the process of rethinking your next career move without having expended too much time or resources.

Action steps

After the initial research and affirmation of the new career path, your next step is to develop an action plan, *How*. A step-by-step guide with timelines and milestones of the specific actions you need to take to get you where you want to be. For example, the following gives you an idea of what actions you may need to plan for, but it is by no means an all-inclusive list of to-do items.

For jobseekers

• Determine what specific role or position you are seeking.

- Do you need to upgrade or acquire new skills? If yes, then when, where, and how.
- Make a list of potential employers to target in the job search.
- Make a list of potential recruiters and agencies to work with.
- Develop several versions of your resume. Do it yourself or with the help of professional resume writers.
- Design an outreach program for your job search – how and when you are proactively going to reach out and connect with potential employers, recruiters, and networking opportunities.
- Create a spreadsheet with goal-setting timelines to track your progress on each of the actions.

For entrepreneurs

- Take stock of your resources – especially monies to sustain yourself and to build your business.
- Do you need additional funding? If so, determine from where and when.
- Do you need to upgrade or acquire new skills? If yes, then when, where, and how.
- Do you need to be licensed or certified? If so, find where you can obtain them.
- Determine the correct legal formation of the business.
- Create a website, blog, and email database.
- Who are your prospective customers or clients?
- How are you going to market your services or products? You must develop a robust marketing plan because without paying customers, there will be no business.

- Do you need to hire employees? When, how many, and where will you find them?
- Create a business plan with goal-setting times for tracking your progress on each of the actions.

A good action plan enables you to map out the various steps you must take to bring your goal to fruition and create a new career. Establishing timelines for accomplishing milestones keeps you motivated and focused on these steps. They serve as useful checklists and reminders of your progress and help you address issues when things are not going as well as envisioned. And yes, things will not always go according to plan.

Plans are, by definition, a roadmap of an intended action and expected outcome. However, actual outcomes are often different. If the plan is not producing the expected results, then go back to the drawing board.

Change the plan, not the goals.

Illustrative example

To demonstrate how this might look like in practice, allow me to continue the story from Chapter 5 – Reinvent to *What*?, after I had the epiphany of changing careers – transitioning from trader to coach. Let me tell you how I researched and planned for my reinvention.

I already had some anecdotal knowledge about the coaching profession, and an intuitive sense, which positively reinforced the idea of becoming a coach. But I needed additional information and sought more clarity before I firmly nailed this idea and committed to it. I started by researching the coaching industry and discovered, as of September 2015:

- The coaching profession continues to evolve and grow – over 53,000 certified coaches worldwide and growing. About 33% were practicing in North America and another 33% in Europe.

- Almost 67% of coaches were female, and more than 50% of all coaches were between the ages of 45 and 59.

- Clients' gender was about 50/50, with approximately 68% of clients between the ages of 35 and 55.

- The estimated 18,000 coaches in North America, on average, earned about $62,000 per year.

- A growing number of individuals and organizations worldwide continued to adopt professional coaching as a key resource for personal and talent development.

- The coaches could be segregated into two broad categories – professionally trained coaches who are accredited and credentialed by one of several professional coaching organizations; and non-certified self-proclaimed coaches.

- The vast majority of clients preferred certified coaches – especially those credentialed by the International Coach Federation (ICF), the industry gold standard. Of the estimated 53,000 coaches worldwide, only about 50% held an ICF credential.

- Coaches were further categorized by specialties – Executive Coach, Leadership Coach, Life Coach, Business Coach, and Career Coach. And these were divided into subcategories.

Future opportunities were growing with increased awareness about the benefits of professional coaching.

Future obstacles were identifying the growing number of untrained individuals posing as coaches, thereby causing marketplace confusion and loss of credibility.

I gathered the aforementioned researched information through several sources – Google searches, industry publications and survey studies, conversations with ICF-certified coaches, and clients utilizing professional coaches. The research process took about three months to complete.

The data affirmed my idea of becoming a coach. However, the analysis also highlighted a few important points for further consideration. To set up for success and become one of the best in the profession, I needed to receive the best available training and become credentialed by the ICF. I wanted to combine my three decades of broad business experience, coupled with my soon-to-be acquired coaching skills, to specialize and focus on a niche market clientele. Attempting to become all things to all potential clients was not a strategy for success.

One data point that was initially discouraging was the survey report claiming the average coach earned only $62,000 per year. Further research revealed that this was a statistical average composed of a majority of coaches offering Life Coaching services, pricing them at the low end. Executive Coaches commanded and were paid at a much higher rate. The old 80/20 rule where 20% of coaches earned 80% of all coaching fees generated held true. I was already leaning toward specializing in Executive Coaching and targeting business leaders as potential clients, and this new information clinched the decision.

All lights were now green, so I moved to the next phase – developing a step-by-step action plan to put myself on the path of becoming a coach. I methodically listed all the action steps that I had to take, when to take them, and the expected timeline for completion.

They looked something like this...

- **Finances:** Every new business launch needs money. I had already done a little back-of-the-envelope math to have an idea of how much capital this startup would need and was comfortable digging into my savings to pay for it. But I needed to budget and plan for expenses in the first 18 months.

- **Coach training and ICF credentialing:** The first and most important thing to do was to acquire new skills and become certified by the most recognized professional body known in the industry for the highest standards. Estimated timeline for training completion and certification: 12 to 18 months.

- **Business formation:** I needed to form an appropriate legal business entity with a suitable name. Timing: At the start of the coach training.

- **Development of a business website:** I wanted to create a robust website to use as both a marketing tool and to capture potential client inquiries. Timing: 3 months from the start of the coach training.

- **Create a marketing plan:** How was I going to get clients? This was the toughest nut to crack. And, the most critical part of any new career. I could have the best skills and a fantastic website, but all that is worth nothing if I could not land clients. I had to think and plan hard on this aspect of the business launch. Timing: 3 to 6 months.

With a plan and these *How* action steps, I was ready to embark on a journey to my new career as an Executive Coach.

Key Takeaways

1. Planning is essential since it serves as a roadmap for the steps you need to take to attain a new career. You cannot get there unless you know where you are going.

2. Before you plan, do a lot of research and gather relevant information about your envisioned new career path.

3. Analyze the research findings, considering your existing resources and skills. Determine if the new career fulfills the basic criteria you set for yourself. Does it require upgrading or training in new skills? Are you up to and committed to the challenge of embarking on this new journey?

4. If the research refutes your initial idea of a career change, now is the time to go back to the drawing board and rethink everything to find clarity.

5. Draw up an action plan of the individual steps you need to take, with corresponding timelines for completion, to execute on your plan to launch your new career.

CHAPTER 7

Executing the Plan

S mart and diligent execution of your plan is the key to success. This is where the rubber meets the road.

Now that you have determined your *Why*, *When*, *What,* and
the *How*, it is time to start implementing your plan, *Execute*.
Even the best-conceived plans amount to nothing unless you put
in the work and do the heavy lifting. Inspired, thoughtful, and
flexible execution is the recipe for success. As you move forward
with the planned action steps, remember this guiding principle.

The plan you conceived is just that, a plan.

It is a snapshot in time of the actions you intended to take.
As you progress, you will most likely discover that not everything is working out as planned. You may encounter obstacles,
uncover new facts, or run into other challenges. Do not throw
up your hands in despair. Such obstacles are to be expected.
Pivot and adapt, tweak, or modify your plan to get around
the real or perceived challenges that you face. Or try another
approach to solve the problem at hand. If you can inspire
yourself by focusing on the reward of ultimately achieving
your goal and continue to persevere, you will succeed.

Another critically important guiding principle as you move on the path to a new career – regardless of whether you are seeking a job or taking the independent entrepreneurial route – is how you market yourself and your services or products.

Notwithstanding how skilled and experienced you are or how good your services and product offerings may be, how you market yourself will make the difference between getting the job you want or the customers you need to attain your goal. Here are a few guiding thoughts on marketing that I find to be universal truisms, and I live by them. If they appeal to you, adopt them.

- **Solve the employers' or customers' problems:** While a prospective employer or customer is interested in your education and experience to assess your skills, they are more interested in knowing whether you can solve *their* problems or fulfill *their* needs. The question they likely have is, "If I hire this person, how will it benefit me?"

- **Integrity:** Be authentic, transparent, and always carry yourself with total integrity, not just when it is convenient. Be honest and stand by your principles.

- **Under promise and over deliver:** In a world where we are continuously disappointed or frustrated with delayed or subpar work, delivering above and beyond on what you promise is a positive surprise that will go a long way in ensuring your success.

With these guiding principles in mind, let us now get started on executing the plan.

Pull out your list of To-Dos, the action steps you prepared for yourself in Chapter 6 – *How* to Plan a Reinvention, and start executing each one of them.

Stay focused, stay disciplined, and stay inspired.

Illustrative example

To demonstrate how this might look in practice, allow me to continue my story from Chapter 6, where I laid out my plan for becoming an Executive Coach.

Financial planning

I created a budget of likely expenses for the next 12 to 18 months – coach training fees, business formation, website development, marketing, travel, and other miscellaneous items. I estimated the total to be around $50,000 to launch the business, not including living expenses. While I would have to dip into my savings to come up with this money, it was unequivocally essential and worth it. I was investing in myself, and I believed in the success of this new career I had chosen.

Coach training

Acquiring coaching skills was the first step toward becoming a coach. As I researched where I could find the appropriate training, I found a plethora of choices, from quick four-week online courses offered by non-accredited providers to full-fledged, intensive curriculum-based coaching programs offered by universities. I wanted the best training I could find and decided on the University of Miami's Certified Professional Coach program.

This was a one-year course taught by renowned faculty members with impressive coaching careers. A few had been instrumental in the founding of the International Coach Federation (ICF), the gold-standard-bearing regulatory body of the coaching profession. Successful completion of this course would enable me to become a Certified Professional Coach and further provide a pathway for becoming a credentialed member of the ICF. I enrolled in this course and started in January 2016.

The program commenced with a two-day in-person orientation and introduction to the program and the other class participants. Subsequent classes were to be conducted twice a week via teleconferencing with follow-on homework assignments requiring about 20 hours of work each week. The class met again for another two-day in-person training at the campus for a mid-year review followed by a final two-day in-person gathering for final exams and graduation in December 2016.

There were 26 participants in my class. The people came from all walks of life – 20 women and 6 men aged from early 30 to mid-50s. I was the oldest at age 65. Did I mention that age does not matter? It was a terrific and diverse group of people. We worked well together – exchanged ideas, helped, and supported each other in developing our own respective coaching niches and practices. And to this day, over four years later, we have stayed connected and check-in to see how we can support each other. Coach training was hard work, but it was also fulfilling and provided for self-reflection and personal improvement.

I had to break some old habits and learn new skills, such as the art of asking powerful questions to enable the coachees to think outside-of-the-box, find clarity around the challenges they faced, and think through potential solutions that would provide the outcomes they were seeking. I learned how powerful the concept of deep listening is, not only as an essential tool in coaching others but also as applied in our daily lives.

The art of powerful questioning and deep listening are two of the most powerful tools in coaching. I recognized early on that mastery of these two techniques – asking powerful questions and deep listening – is what differentiates ordinary coaches from the great ones. I worked hard at honing these skills – researching, thinking creatively, experimenting, and practicing. To this day, I continue to learn and work on improving my coaching skills.

Coach training was intensive and time-consuming. I suspect that I made it so by getting fully immersed in it with an all-in approach of becoming the best. This provided a lot of intellectual stimulation and got the creative juices flowing. If there was a concept that I did not quite grasp or a skill that I had not yet mastered, I sought help – asked questions, did research, and worked hard at it – until I became highly proficient.

With respect to learning new skills and the reinvention process, I was on a high, totally immersed and invigorated. But there were moments of doubt on the business end – specifically, how would I procure clients? As with most professional service providers like doctors, attorneys, and coaches, clients prefer to engage the more experienced and reputable coaches. I was a new coach with little formal coaching experience and no street credibility. It was a chicken-and-egg situation. I knew that my business background and expertise trumped many of the big-name coaches out there. Some had been coaching their entire careers without ever having run a business or solved real-world issues in a business setting, while others had transitioned into coaching from the human resource/talent training disciplines. But I had to overcome the perceived lack of 'coaching experience' when marketing myself. This is what kept me up at night, thinking creatively about the challenge of acquiring clients.

In December 2016, I graduated as a Certified Professional Coach from the University of Miami. Not long after that, I received accreditation by the ICF with the highly sought-after credential of Professional Certified Coach (PCC).

Formed a company

I consulted with my accountant for a suitable legal structure for my coaching practice, and together, we determined that the LLC classification was the most appropriate for my business. The next hurdle was naming the business. In March 2016, while I was still in coach training, I formed Chopra Coaching LLC.

As a professional service provider, the name of the newly formed coaching business needed to convey clear information to a prospective client as to what the business offered – coaching services. Hence, 'Coaching' needed to be in my company's name. Since coaching is a personal thing, I wanted to add my last name, Chopra, to the business name to signify the provider of the coaching services. Thus, Chopra Coaching was founded. Of course, it did not hurt to have Chopra in the business name, considering that there is another popularly famous Chopra who is a household name – Dr. Deepak Chopra, author of many books and an influential advocate for alternative medicine and mind-body healing.

Developed a website

Concurrently with the business formation, I hired a website developer and built a purposeful and robust website, www.chopracoaching.com, for my coaching practice.

The site provides information on my coaching service offerings, coaching values and process, and information on how to contact me and schedule a consultation. In addition, it offers other useful information to visitors and potential clients to determine if I am the coach best-suited to their needs:

- Information on my personal background and business experience.

- My ideal potential clients – executives, managers, and investment professionals.
- What clients can expect – the coaching process and coach/client relationship.
- How I coach – my coaching philosophy and customized approach for each client.
- Why I coach.
- Why choose me as a coach – what differentiates me from other coaches.

The website also provides blog articles and client testimonials that visitors may find useful. For many potential customers, the site is the first place they go to research whether I might be the right coach for them.

Created a marketing plan

Without a doubt, this is the hardest part of launching a business. How does one find paying clients? Coaches like attorneys, doctors, and other professional service providers typically get clients through personal referrals. And because of the highly confidential and intimate relationship that develops between a coach and client, executive coaches are more dependent on referrals. While skills matter, the single-most-important factor above all else is the client's trust in the coach. The coach must have integrity, empathy, and be truly authentic. With the trust factor in mind, I had to craft a marketing strategy that would work for a new coach, like me, to secure clients.

Soon after I developed the website, I began tapping my network – friends and some prior business associates – and offered them pro bono coaching sessions. This did a few good things. It put out the word that I was now in the coaching business, and the real-life sessions helped me hone my coaching skills.

I started to write and publish articles on LinkedIn, in investment journals, and on my website blog to target potential clients – business leaders, investment professionals, and entrepreneurs – on topics that they might find useful in the development of their leadership and business skills. I engaged a public relations and marketing firm to help grow awareness of my coaching services. As a result of the PR efforts, I found several speaking engagements at various conferences, universities, and non-profit organizations; participated in podcasts; and was interviewed and written up in major newspapers, e.g., the *Miami Herald*, and other publications. I did all this to build awareness of my coaching practice and grow a network of potential client prospects.

In the summer of 2016, while I was still in coach training, I met with an old friend, Sandeep Mathrani, who at the time was the CEO of General Growth Partners (GGP), a real estate investment trust (REIT) that owned shopping mall properties in the U.S. After the financial crisis of 2008, GGP suffered massive losses and filed for bankruptcy. In 2011, Sandeep was hired to become the CEO to restructure the business and turn it around. Sandeep did an amazing job. By 2016, he had turned the company into a huge profit-making business, with a market value of over $25 billion and inclusion as an S&P 500 company. This great turnaround story, going from bankruptcy to becoming the second-largest shopping mall owner in the U.S. in five years, was all because of Sandeep's vision, expertise, and the operational execution of the amazing team of professionals at GGP.

Our meeting was purely a personal and social get-to-gether. As the dinner conversation drifted to how I was now engaged in Executive Coaching, he made me an offer, "Why don't you come and coach our team?" I was surprised and thrilled beyond belief. To get an offer like this from a superstar executive left me speechless. "Look, we are a very forward-looking company with a culture of learning and want to grow our people and their leadership skills for the future. Come work as a coach with my team for six months, and then we'll see how it goes," Sandeep said. This is my lucky break, I thought. I had just landed my first significant coaching client, even before I had completed my coach training program. This was totally unexpected, and it was indeed a lucky break. The coaching engagement with GGP began with an initial term of six months, which was later extended to a period lasting over three years. During that term, I coached over 150 executives and professionals at GGP, including the entire C-Suite executive team, senior officers, middle managers, and aspiring young professionals at the company. I am forever grateful for the opportunity he gave me. That was the steppingstone I needed.

From there, I focused my marketing efforts on reaching out to build relationships with similar high-profile companies where I could potentially land coaching engagements.

Marketing is hard work and often frustrating. But professional service providers have no choice but to continuously engage in it to grow their business.

But the execution of the plan does not stop here. *Execute* is an ongoing process that continues to evolve and is the subject of the next chapter. I continue to work on it every day, and so should you.

Key Takeaways

1. Execution of your plan is the key to success. Be determined, yet stay flexible in adapting and changing your plan when necessary.

2. Embrace integrity in all your actions.

3. Execution of your plan requires hard work. Stay inspired, focused, and determined. When in doubt, check your compass and rethink solutions when faced with challenges to get around obstacles.

4. Create a mindset of "under promise and over deliver."

5. Define your value proposition to prospective employers or customers. How will *they* benefit from hiring you?

CHAPTER 8

When Reinvention Succeeds

So, you have successfully executed your plan to reinvent your career and arrived at the place where you wanted to be. Congratulations!

What do you do next?

This is your new career and a new life. You have completed the first leg of the journey and now need to embark on another – a continuous series of actions to build and grow your new career.

There is much more work to do.

Illustrative example

You have transitioned from being employed by a large company to starting your own solo-practitioner consulting business. Examine your business model. Is it set up for success? In addition to the administrative aspects of operating your consulting practice and servicing existing clients, there are two critical components that you need to focus on – client acquisitions and new learning.

Client acquisitions

Who are your target clients, and how are you going to get them to hire you? The first step is to identify your ideal potential clients. Since your consulting business is limited to a finite number of client billing hours, you must determine the following at the outset:

- **Type of clients:** Determine if your clients will be institutional or individuals, and identify any specific industry or service sector.

- **How many clients:** Given the limited number of hours you have at your disposal, how many client engagements can you handle productively?

- **Billing rate:** What are you going to charge clients for your services? How does it compare with your competitors? Does the amount that you charge for your consulting service (hourly, daily, or fixed fee) times the number of clients add up to your desired financial goals?

Clarity about client type, number of clients, and the billing rate are essential for your business model to be programmed for success. For example, having many clients paying lower fees adds diversification to the client base, where the loss of one client may not materially impact your business. However, it requires acquiring a lot of clients. Having fewer high-paying clients likely makes you more productive and elevates your market 'going rate' for consulting engagements. But this runs the risk that losing a single client may adversely impact your business. It is a trade-off and warrants considerable thought.

Once you identify your potential clients and how many you can work with simultaneously, develop a marketing strategy for how to generate and close on client leads.

Revisit the plan you developed for yourself in Chapter 6 – *How* to Plan a Reinvention.

Examine your marketing strategy. Does it include and clearly communicate the following items to potential clients?

- **Your client-focused value proposition:** Explain what you can do for them, which of their problems you can help them solve, and how *they* will benefit from hiring you.

- **What you do:** It should also clearly articulate *what* you do, *how* you do it, and *why* you do it.

- **How you are different:** Think about skills, experience, market reputation, client responsiveness, integrity, and other attributes that differentiate you from your competitors.

- **Why a potential client should hire you:** Yes, the preceding points above already include elements of why a client might hire you, but it helps to articulate a clear and concise 'elevator pitch' to convey the differentiating reason.

Marketing and client acquisition in service-oriented businesses like consulting is a long game. It is a process of outreach, creating awareness, planting seeds, and building relationships.

You must stay focused and execute diligently.

If you discover that a part of your marketing execution – for example, a social media outreach campaign – did not produce the desired outcomes, then adjust your marketing plan and pivot to find another way of achieving better results.

New learning

Since you transitioned from being an employee to a business owner, there is likely a steep learning curve. Learning how to operate a business is one part, and delivering high level service to clients is the other. The former is easier since many administrative tasks of running a business can be economically outsourced to third-party vendors. The latter, delivering high-quality services, may require you to upgrade your skills, such as formal training classes, to perhaps gain new subject matter expertise. Participate in industry-specific conferences and webinars to learn and stay abreast of new methods and best practices. Utilize other relevant techniques to keep up to date on the current developments in your chosen field.

While the previous example highlighted the transition from working for an employer to going into business for yourself, a similar approach also applies to those who reinvent themselves from one job to another in a different field, industry, or role. The new learning component is likely applicable in the new position.

The Day 1 mindset

Finding initial success after your reinvention is sweet, but you should not rest on your laurels. Success is a long game, and you must remain focused and continue executing your best as if it were Day 1. Adopt the Day 1 mindset.

What is the Day 1 mindset?

Jeff Bezos is a genius. According to *Forbes* magazine, he is also one of the smartest, most successful entrepreneurs ever, having founded Amazon and become the world's richest man with a net worth of $161 billion. Among the thousands of brilliant decisions that likely made Amazon so successful, there is one that stands out – Amazon espousing the Day 1 mindset.

The following are excerpts from a recent letter from Jeff Bezos to Amazon's shareholders where he explains what Day 1 means:

"'Jeff, what does Day 2 look like?'

"That's a question I just got at our most recent all-hands meeting. I've been reminding people that it's Day 1 for a couple of decades. I work in an Amazon building named Day 1, and when I moved buildings, I took the name with me. I spend time thinking about this topic.

"'Day 2 is stasis. Followed by irrelevance. Followed by excruciating, painful decline. Followed by death. And that is why it is always Day 1.'

"To be sure, this kind of decline would happen in extreme slow motion. An established company might harvest Day 2 for decades, but the result would still come.

"I'm interested in the question, how do you fend off Day 2? What are the techniques and tactics? How do you keep the vitality of Day 1, even inside a large organization?

"Such a question can't have a simple answer. There will be many elements, multiple paths, and many traps. I don't know the whole answer, but I may know bits of it. Here's a starter pack of essentials for Day 1 defense:

customer obsession, a skeptical view of proxies, the eager adoption of external trends, and high-velocity decision making.

"Staying in Day 1 requires you to experiment patiently, accept failures, plant seeds, protect saplings, and double down when you see customer delight. A customer-obsessed culture best creates the conditions where all of that can happen."

So, to continue being successful, the mantra is that every day is like Day 1 of your reinvention. Day 2 should never arrive.

Illustrative example 2

Continuing with the story in Chapter 7 – Executing the Plan, this is what I did, and I continue to engage in growing my coaching practice every day as if it were Day 1.

I received a lucky break and landed my first significant coaching engagement with a large corporate client (GGP) to coach its executives. The agreement was to provide one-on-one in-person coaching for two weeks each month at GGP's head office in Chicago for an initial period of six months. I lived in Miami, so every other week, I flew from Miami to Chicago and engaged in coaching about 15 to 20 GGP executives each week. Upon return to Miami after each visit, I typically spent time reviewing the coaching work I had done and doing related follow-up work. There was just a little time left over before I prepped for my next visit the following week.

However, I recognized that I had to start growing my client base since one cannot build a sustainable business around just one client. Coaching engagements have a finite life, and at some point, they will end. Therefore, it was essential to develop a pipeline of additional clients. I began to actively market my coaching services using a multi-pronged strategy.

Identified potential target clients, both companies and individual professionals, in the financial services and investments/wealth management businesses – banks, brokerage firms, asset management companies, hedge funds, and private equity firms. I understood the challenges these professionals face in their careers because I had experienced them myself. With a deep understanding of their businesses and over two decades of experience as a trader, I could provide valuable coaching and guidance to these finance and trading professionals.

Launched an outreach campaign to connect with senior professionals at the targeted firms through the LinkedIn platform. In terms of generating client interest, it yielded less than what I was hoping, but it created awareness of my name among 3,000 LinkedIn members.

Started to write and publish articles in professional journals, LinkedIn, and my blog on topics related to leadership, how coaching can enhance performance, and other subject matters that are of interest to finance professionals and executives.

Hired a public relations professional who helped me secure major newspaper and podcast interviews, speaking engagements at alternative investment conferences, universities, and other venues. And I launched a pro-bono financial literacy coaching program at a non-profit charity for underprivileged children.

Engaged in new learning about best practices by researching new thought leadership ideas pertaining to coaching. I read extensively, participated in webinars, and had discussions with other leading coaches.

While I was executing on client acquisition, the GGP engagement was extended beyond the initial six months and lasted over three years. My dilemma during that engagement was that I did not have available time to handle another large corporate client. Still, I continued to work on client development to build relationships with potential future clients.

Some aspects of the initial marketing strategy worked well, while others did not, especially the email campaign on LinkedIn. However, I learned what did not work and tweaked and modified my client development focus more on personal introductions and referrals.

Yes, it is now four years since I launched my coaching practice, and it is still Day 1.

Key Takeaways

1. Having arrived at your new career is only the beginning of your new journey.

2. There is a lot more work to do to make the reinvention sustainably successful.

3. Adopt the mindset that each day is Day 1.

4. For jobseekers, you must grow your new career by focusing on new learning and skills development.

5. For independents and entrepreneurs, focus on both client development and new learning.

CHAPTER 9

When Reinvention Fails

Often in life, even our utmost efforts in executing the best plan do not yield the outcomes that we seek. The world has conditioned us to believe that our actions result in binary outcomes like success or failure. Personally, I do not espouse that belief. For me, there are, in an abstract sense, no successes or failures – only good or bad outcomes or good or bad experiences. Sometimes, we may make the right decisions that result in bad outcomes, and at other times, we may make poor decisions that result in good outcomes. So, when faced with a seeming reinvention failure, it is inspiring to recall this story of historical significance.

"At around 5:30 in the evening on Dec. 10, 1914, a massive explosion erupted in West Orange, New Jersey. Ten buildings in legendary inventor Thomas Edison's plant, which made up more than half of the site, were engulfed in flames. Between six and eight fire departments rushed to the scene, but the chemical-fueled inferno was too powerful to put out quickly.

"According to a 1961 Reader's Digest *article by Edison's son Charles, Edison calmly walked over to Charles*

as he watched the fire destroy his dad's work. In a child-like voice, Edison told his 24-year-old son, 'Go get your mother and all her friends. They'll never see a fire like this again.' When Charles objected, Edison said, 'It's all right. We've just got rid of a lot of rubbish.'

"Later, at the scene of the blaze, Edison was quoted in The New York Times *as saying, 'Although I am over 67 years old, I'll start all over again tomorrow.' He told the reporter that he was exhausted from remaining at the scene until the chaos was under control, but he stuck to his word and immediately began rebuilding the next morning without firing any of his employees.*

"But after just three weeks, with a sizable loan from his friend Henry Ford, Edison got part of the plant up and running again. His employees worked double shifts and set to work producing more than ever. Edison and his team went on to make almost $10 million in revenue the following year."

— *Business Insider*

If the attempt to reinvent fails, what do you do?

The first step is to recognize the fact that the effort did not produce the desired outcome. To be sure, it is difficult, but we must acknowledge and accept it. Living in denial is not productive. The second step is to determine the personal impact of this failure. Is the disappointment emotionally destabilizing, causing immense frustration or desperation? Dig deep into your inner self and muster all the courage, strength, and inspiration that only you know how to garner emotional stability.

Surround yourself with people who care about you. Share the experiences with your tribe or others who are a positive force in your life and are supportive. Consider the impact on your finances and shore them up as best you can. Find a coach or mentor and regroup, rethink, and move forward.

The next step is to examine, with brutal honesty, why the reinvention failed. Discovering and understanding what went wrong provides new knowledge for the future.

---

*We learn more from our mistakes
than from our successes.*

Here are a few possible reasons why an effort to reinvent might fail:

- The **why** was not the true why,
- The **what** was wrong,
- The **plan** was flawed,
- The **execution** was poor, or
- **Exogenous events** negatively impacted the plan and/or its execution.

Were the *why* and the *what* incorrectly determined?

Look back to the time when you determined *why* you wanted to reinvent your career. Review your thinking and true motivation as to why you wanted to reinvent. Analyze your notes and the Key Takeaways from Chapter 2 – *Why* Reinvent Yourself. Ask yourself if the reasoning is still valid. Or did something change, such as the rationale itself, or did your motivation and enthusiasm wane?

Similarly, evaluate the process of determining the *what* of your reinvention. Did you have total clarity of the objective? Was the transformation or transitioning into the new career deemed realistic and feasible? Refer to Chapter 5 – Reinvent to *What*? to review and analyze your thinking and assumptions and see if they are still valid.

Was the plan flawed at inception?

Honestly and deeply analyze and determine if the plan, and the underlying assumptions, were well thought out. Were the goals realistic? Did you have adequate resources available as required by the plan, e.g., sufficient finances, new skills training, and a good marketing plan? With the benefit of hindsight, would you now go back and make any changes to the original strategy?

This learning could either provide the catalyst to fix what went wrong and save success from the jaws of failure or provide a good learning experience for the future.

Was the execution poor?

Did you really give your 100 percent effort when executing the plan? Did you proactively seek and find solutions to challenges as they came your way? Did you, at any time, simply resign and give up? If you were to start all over again, what would you do differently?

These questions help you find the mistakes, if any, that were made. Recognizing mistakes helps us learn and grow, and often prompts us into taking remedial action to make right that which has gone wrong.

Was the failure due to exogenous events?

Sometimes, exogenous events like a business shutdown caused by a pandemic can throw us into failure. While the loss from such a failure can be enormous, recognize that exogenous events are those that are beyond your control. There is not much you can do when you do not have control over the circumstances.

What do you do next?

Regroup. Get yourself back up on your feet. If you are short of money, find a job, *any job*, that will help stabilize your finances and give you time to rethink your future. And rethink you must. Be creative and start to map out a new plan to achieve your goal. Did I mention: If the plan does not work, change the plan, not the goal.

However, and this is a big caveat, if your goal has changed, then of course, you need to revise the plan. It is entirely possible that in your journey of reinvention, you might discover that the goal you initially established is no longer valid or exogenous events have rendered attainment of the goal as no longer desirable or achievable. In instances like this, abandon the goal and/or start afresh with the reinvention process.

Illustrative example

Back in the late 1990s, there was a revolution in the telecommunications industry.

The internet had been created, and the dot.com craze was booming. There was a mind-blowing demand for internet access, especially high-speed access to deliver ever-increasing volumes of content. The old copper wire phone networks of the traditional telecom providers like Verizon and AT&T were not designed for this, so there was inadequate bandwidth in the existing infrastructure.

Seizing the opportunity, many new entrepreneurial companies emerged to build the new telecom infrastructure – the fiber-optic and wireless networks. There were literally hundreds of business startups that emerged during this period to provide broadband access to businesses and consumers. The demand, and the anticipated future demand, for broadband was insatiable. Companies like Level 3 Communications, Global Crossing, and RCN, to name a few, rapidly started building vast fiber-optic networks deploying tens of billions of dollars. Level 3 Communications laid the cross-country fiber-optic pipes, Global Crossing focused on laying undersea fiber-optic cables, and RCN concentrated on building the 'last mile' networks.

In October 1997, I met David McCourt, a charismatic and brilliant entrepreneur and founder of RCN. We both lived in Princeton, New Jersey, and soon became friends. We enjoyed exchanging big picture ideas and each other's company. He would share his thoughts on the emergence of the internet and the technological innovation of fiber optics and delivery of content over broadband networks. At that time, I was working as a derivatives trader at JPMorgan Chase and would share my insights on financial innovation, such as the emergence of online banking and the potential opportunities for new startup banks. One morning over coffee during our customary chats, David said to me, "Raj, I think you're wasting your fucking life working on Wall Street. There's a telecom revolution going on, and I'm leading the charge. I think you should quit your job and come work with me. We're going to change the world, make it a better place, and get rich in the process." I was flattered by the offer and surely intrigued by the potential of RCN changing the telecom industry. I said to him, "Dave, I'm a derivatives trader, a Wall Street money guy, I understand banking, finance, and markets but don't know a thing about telecom...and not sure how I could add value." To which he responded, "Hey, I didn't know anything about telecom either. I came from the construction industry. We'll learn together. You're a smart guy. I need smart people, and we'll learn and figure it out as we build the company." David can be extremely persuasive. I was sold, excited by the prospect of blazing an entirely new career. In early 1998, I left my trading job at JPMorgan Chase and joined the telecom revolution as President of Business Development at RCN.

At that time, the telecom industry was growing exponentially. Investors had drunk the kool-aid, and Wall Street was throwing money, big money, at any company that had anything to do with fiber-optic networks or had dot.com in its name. Between 1996 and 2000, over a trillion dollars was deployed to construct fiber-optic and wireless networks. Investor demand for a piece of the action was voracious, and company valuations, including RCN, soared into the stratosphere. This was a market bubble, I thought. In meetings with potential business partners and acquisition candidates, it was sometimes unclear to either party whether they would be writing a check or receiving one. This was insanity. Years of experience trading the markets had taught me one thing – recognize investor madness when you see it. I knew this was going to end badly.

Soon, there was a large surplus of network capacity, and the price of saleable bandwidth began to fall. Subsequently, the dot.com bubble burst, and bandwidth prices collapsed even further along with the valuations of literally hundreds of telecom upstarts. Absent investor demand, the capital pipeline dried up, and many of the network infrastructure firms went bankrupt.

After the failure of the fiber-optic network providers, I was approached by a leading Wall Street derivatives broker-age firm, Prebon Yamane, to start a bandwidth derivatives brokerage business.

The idea was compelling. The bandwidth trading market was in its infancy, comprised primarily of bandwidth providers (the network owners) and end-users, with no intermediaries or market makers to provide price discovery and liquidity. Additionally, there were no derivative instruments with which the buyers and sellers could hedge against rising or falling prices. To get in on the ground floor and create an entirely new market for derivatives and risk management – think of the intellectual and financial rewards – was the most exciting opportunity I had seen. It fit my DNA because I had the deriv-atives trading experience and the new telecom insights and contacts. So, I signed on to start this venture.

In January 2001, I co-founded Prebon Bandwidth as a divi-sion of the parent company Prebon Yamane, which provided the capital and office space. I hired a small team of expert talent – a former derivatives trading colleague, a telecom engineer, and an analyst/broker. Our plan was simple: Create bandwidth derivatives instruments that help market partici-pants hedge their price risk, and then bring in buyers and sellers to transact in those derivatives. We made our money by taking a fee for structuring and arranging the transaction.

We were up and running in a few months after the start day. The biggest traders, our primary customers, were surpris-ingly not the telecom networks, but the energy companies led by Enron. Remember that Enron – the smartest guys in the room – was the big energy company that went belly up after the uncovering of massive fraud. Enron entered the bandwidth trading business in a big way, believing that it was just like trading energy or other commodities, to grab a dominant position in this emerging market.

Our brokerage business looked very promising, and we were making significant inroads into the bandwidth trading markets, and then suddenly, it all began to unravel. Enron was getting caught up in a scandal of fraud and ceased its bandwidth trading activities. Soon after that, the remaining bandwidth trading houses followed suit. The bandwidth trading business came to a grinding halt, and toward the end of 2002, so did the future of Prebon Bandwidth.

My team and I were devasted. All our hard work had gone to waste, and our business had failed. It failed because of an exogenous event that triggered the collapse of an entire market.

What did I do?

I accepted the bad outcome for what it was. The business had failed, and I was out of a job. I regrouped and rethought my career. This was a setback, not a death sentence, but I had to shore up my lost income. I had to find a job to stabilize myself and allow other new opportunities to emerge.

So, I pounded on Wall Street doors and found a job trading and brokering interest rate derivatives. A lesser job, with lower income than I had previously at JPMorgan Chase, but it provided income and time to rethink my next career move.

Key Takeaways

1. Accept a bad outcome as a fact. Do not be in denial when the effort to reinvent fails. It is a setback but not a death sentence.

2. Stabilize your emotions. Seek support from those who care about you. Seek the counsel of a mentor or those who can be helpful.

3. Shore up your finances. If money is tight, find a job – any job – that will support you until you figure out your next gig.

4. Analyze with brutal honesty why you failed. Was it a flawed plan, poor execution, or an exogenous event?

5. Explore what you could have done differently that would have averted failure. We learn from our mistakes. Take this as a learning lesson for the future.

6. Regroup. Rethink. Continue pursuing your goal. Do not let one failed attempt derail or demoralize you.

CHAPTER 10

Conclusion

Technological innovation has introduced an era of rapid and creative disruption. It has reshaped industries and the global economy. Exogenous events often accelerate the evolution of how we work and live.

Millions of old jobs and careers have been adversely impacted or risk becoming extinct in the future. New products and services are being created to meet the demands of the future 'new normal.' Therefore, to succeed in the evolving change, we need to rethink, reimagine, and reinvent ourselves. What worked in the past may not work well in the future. We must adapt and transform to remain relevant and find success and fulfillment in our careers. We need to become agile, especially in midlife and midcareer.

We must change, or change will be forced upon us.

While many people may recognize the need to reinvent themselves, they are often stumped by the daunting "I don't know how" syndrome. Hence this book.

As you read in the preceding chapters, reinvention is not difficult when you commit to remake yourself, but it requires hard work and determination. You must become *Stoic*. One of the best definitions of *Stoic* that I have read is from Nassim Nicholas Taleb, the philosopher, author, and market observer. He defines a *Stoic* as someone who "transforms fear into prudence, pain into transformation, mistakes into initiation and desire into undertaking."

We must be *Stoic* when it comes to reinventing our careers. If you recognize the need for change, I encourage you to be bold and courageous. Go for it.

In the book, I identified and described the logical steps to remake your career:

- Determine your *Why* for reinvention.
- Find clarity on *What* you want to reinvent to.
- Develop a *Plan.*
- Execute the *Plan*.
- When reinvention succeeds, there is still more work to do.
- Analyze and regroup when the attempt to reinvent fails.

If you are stuck in your current career, fear losing your job, or have lost one recently and are contemplating a career change – act. Do not let inertia hold you back. And if you are in midlife, I hope you can draw some insights and inspiration from my experience of reinventions – I am still doing it at age 69 by becoming a first-time book author. If I can do it, anyone can.

If this book helps you in your journey, then nobody would be more gratified than me.

Additional guidance and resources are provided on my website: **www.chopracoaching.com**.

Readers, if you found this book helpful, please go to Amazon or wherever you bought it and write an honest review. I thank you for that.

*I would love to hear your comments, and if I can help coach or guide you in your career in any way, please reach out to me at **rajan@chopracoaching.com**.*

Author Bio

Rajan Chopra is a former Wall Street derivatives trader and entrepreneur turned executive coach, author, and motivational speaker. He helps C-suite and mid-level executives, investment professionals, entrepreneurs, and other high achievers in career reinvention, leadership development, disruptive change management, and business strategy.

rajan@chopracoaching.com
www.chopracoaching.com